"You CAN safely invest for your retirement. An excellent read if you are planning for retirement and are just not sure how to make it all work. The author's explanation of the primary investment products available to potential retirees was easy to understand and provided what I needed to choose among the options. As a bonus, the author included an appendix of financial terms and their meanings. Highly recommended!"

"Outstanding information and book. I read Tim's first book twice and refer to it as a great reminder of key principles. This second book is great and packed full of awesome information."

"Easy to understand, thoroughly explains retirement options. This is an excellent book. Tim clearly lays out options in language a client can understand. I highly recommend it."

"Best handbook available on what to do with your401K"

SHOULD I BUY AN ANNUITY?

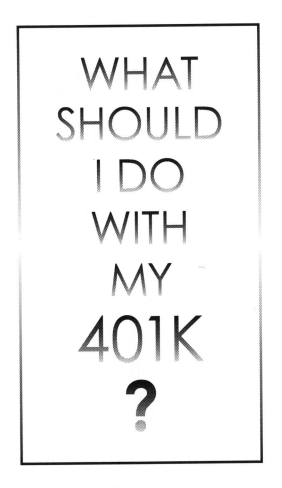

WHAT
SHOULD
I DO
WITH
MY
401K
?

TIM CLAIRMONT

WHAT SHOULD I DO WITH MY 401K ?
SHOULD I BUY AN ANNUITY?

Securities are offered through ClearFP Securities, LLC, member FINRA & SIPC. Investment Advisory Services are offered through ClearFP Advisors, LLC. ClearFP Securities, LLC and ClearFP Advisors, LLC are wholly owned subsidiaries of Clear Financial Partners, Inc.

The information, ideas, and suggestions in this book are not intended to render professional advice. Before following any suggestions contained in this book, you should consult your personal accountant or other financial advisor. Neither the author nor the publisher shall be liable or responsible for any loss or damage allegedly arising as a consequence of your use or application of any information or suggestions in this book.

iUniverse books may be ordered through booksellers or by contacting:

iUniverse
1663 Liberty Drive
Bloomington, IN 47403
www.iuniverse.com
844-349-9409

Because of the dynamic nature of the Internet, any web addresses or links contained in this book may have changed since publication and may no longer be valid. The views expressed in this work are solely those of the author and do not necessarily reflect the views of the publisher, and the publisher hereby disclaims any responsibility for them.

Any people depicted in stock imagery provided by Getty Images are models, and such images are being used for illustrative purposes only. Certain stock imagery © Getty Images.

ISBN: 978-1-5320-7591-9 (sc)
ISBN: 978-1-5320-7590-2 (e)

Library of Congress Control Number: 2019907573

Print information available on the last page.

iUniverse rev. date: 01/12/2024

CONTENTS

PREFACE

When I wrote this book in 2018, I had no idea that it would reach Amazon #1 best-seller status. I also didn't realize that Amazon would become an even bigger goliath in the imminent COVID crisis as many quarantined Americans relied on in-home deliveries to weather the storm. And, I had no idea that we would see such a powerful bull market run continue through 2018, 2019, 2020, and 2021. Nor did I know that we would see the recent bear market downturn from June of 2022 to June of 2023.

Now, we find ourselves in the last half of 2023 still experiencing rising interest rates as the Fed combats some of the most severe inflation we've seen in forty years.

Things have changed since I wrote What Should I Do with My 401k? But, in many ways, the insights in these pages are timeless.

Annuities have only increased in popularity since 2018. The SECURE ACT of 2019 became law one year after this book was originally published, and we are now beginning to see annuities actually offered inside 401k plans.

While the annuities you will see inside your 401k plans are very different from those available outside your 401k, it is abundantly clear that retirees want more income that is guaranteed to last as long as they live. And, with inflation picking up, they want rising income.

This text has been updated to reflect the five years that have transpired since it's original publishing. Surprisingly, very few changes were necessary. Even in this post-COVID, high inflation era the biggest edits came from the legislative implementation of the SECURE ACT of 2019 and the subsequent December 2022 legislation of the SECURE ACT 2.0. With these legislative changes, we now have even more room in our 401k's!

With all of this in mind, I hope you enjoy this book for what it is. This is a basic introduction to the traditional investment choices available to 401k investors. This isn't the complete answer to the question What Should I Do with My 401k? I won't tell you what to do; you will have to make that final decision. This is, however, enough information for most people to narrow their focus as they choose their own answers to the question – **WHAT SHOULD I DO WITH MY 401K?**

DEDICATION

This book is dedicated to all of my clients. Without you, I never would have made it this far. Thank you for your loyalty, your friendship, your commitment, and your trust.

INTRODUCTION

Annuity is one of the most controversial words in the United States. If you google the word *annuity*, you will find passionate anti-annuity blogs and messages proclaiming that annuities are horrible investment vehicles, yet this investment continues to grow in popularity across the country.

Why the disconnect? Why do wise investors continue to invest in annuity contracts?

This book addresses these questions. As a Certified Financial Planner who has served retiring baby boomers for more than twenty-five years, Tim Clairmont is well versed in the multitude of investment options that face our retirees.

As a fiduciary to his clients, Tim is required by law and by moral code to put his clients' best interests ahead of his own. He *must* offer to help his clients do what is in *their* best interests.

Over the past two decades, we have all experienced tremendous losses in the stock market and frustration with a volatile economy. These decades began with the peak of an eighteen-year-long bull market run in the stock market in the late '90s. Then...the uneventful Y2K was followed by the tech bubble crash in March of 2000. A little more than a year later, our nation mourned over 9/11, and our stock market and economy took two more years to recover. This three-year attack on our 401k balances obliterated the retirement values that many soon-to-be retirees were counting on to carry them forward into their golden years. Following those dismal three years, we started to climb our way back out of the hole we had dug. Then, just as 401k balances started to recover and investors poked their heads out of their turtle shells—*blam!*—the financial crisis of 2008 wiped out investor confidence yet again.

As many investors continued to buy and hold and ride through this lost decade, other investors jumped ship from modern portfolio theory. They reached for the shiny life preserver of *tactical* investment strategies in the hope that this new way of investing would keep them on the predicted trajectory of growth they were banking on during the early 2000s. Of course, this strategy embraced various means of timing the market, but they didn't quite use the words *timing the market.* (After all, clients had already learned that market timing was a bad idea in the '90s, so why would the new style of tactical investing ever reveal that it was just another name for market timing?)

Now, over a decade has gone by since the financial crisis of 2008. Shell-shocked baby boomers are starting to poke their heads out once more, but they can't afford another lost decade. And the question they are all asking is: *What Should I Do With My 401k?*

Since the late '90s, Tim has used a proprietary education-based approach to teach clients about all their investment options.[1] Through his continuous study of annuities, managed money, and all the other traditional (and many nontraditional) means of investing, Tim became extremely knowledgeable in the breadth of options available to the investing public. By focusing his services on baby boomers, Tim has learned the unique goals, dreams, and passions of thousands of Americans all over the United States. Moreover, he has dedicated his career to the service of this particular group of people.

With the knowledge and wisdom he has obtained, Tim filters it down to this easy-to-read explanation that answers the question: *What Should I Do With My 401k?*

In this book, Tim will share with you the facts and circumstances behind annuities, managed money, mutual funds, ETFs, and the limited array of options for the investment of your 401k plan.

As you approach or enter retirement, you face a critical decision. Making a mistake is not an option. Use this book to get a clear view of the investment landscape from a veteran fiduciary who puts his clients' interests ahead of everyone else's.

---

[1] You can learn more about his approach by downloading the free educational app: *ClearFP: The Clock.*

THE ENVIRONMENT

More people were born in the United States in 1957 than in any other year in US history.

Why is that significant? Because that means that we have more people turning sixty-five years old than ever before. More importantly, when it comes to your 401k, we have more people who have recently reached the magic age of fifty-nine and a half than ever before.

Why is *fifty-nine and a half* a significant age? Because that is the age at which investors can touch their 401k, IRA, and other qualified retirement plans without paying the 10 percent penalty tax to the Internal Revenue Service. Yep, that's right. You can touch your retirement money without a tax penalty once you reach the age of fifty-nine and a half. In fact, most qualified retirement plan accounts don't even require you to be retired. You can usually take an *in-service distribution* once you have a qualifying event. One of those qualifying events for most 401k plans is reaching the age of fifty-nine and a half.

So, here we are. Our firm's average client was born between the early 1950s and the mid 1960s. These clients were in their teens and early twenties during the times of disco and the acoustic-guitar-playing storytellers. They were taught in school by a teacher with a chalkboard. They followed the rules because they were raised around parents and grandparents who had survived the Great Depression and TWO World Wars.

They worked hard as they raised their kids through the '80s. They saved in this new thing called a 401k because it was there, and because the pensions that used to be there were starting to vanish.

Their kids were raised watching *Family Ties* and *Family Matters*. They listened and fell in love with *New Kids on the Block*, *Madonna*, and *Paula Abdul*. The computer revolution came and raised the balances of their 401k's from the early '80s all the way through the '90s.

They saw paper money growing at an amazing rate, but they knew they shouldn't touch it. It was retirement money. And they followed the rules.

The rules also said, "Leave that money alone when the market goes down. You've got to ride it through." And that is what many of them did. Some of their friends bailed and moved their money to cash when the market was down. They lost a ton, and they probably still complain about it to this day. Other friends bragged about getting out of the market just in time. Of course, many of them are still out and are waiting for "just the right time" to get back in. Unsure of what to do, most of these baby boomers just did nothing. They let the money in their 401k sit right where it was. They followed the rules and rode the money down in the early 2000s and back up again between 2003 and 2007. Then, they were tested again in 2008. Many of them did the same thing. Some bailed. Some bragged. Most just rode through.

And now, where does that leave us? Most of the investing public is sitting on hundreds of thousands of dollars or, in many cases, millions of dollars in these special accounts we affectionately call *401k*.

Now, these same good citizens, these same hardworking, loyal Americans, are faced with a daunting decision as they near and enter retirement: What do I do with my money?

WHAT NOW?

Well, before we can tell you what to do with your money, we have to answer the most important question: *What do you want?*

Of course, no one seems to *really* know the answer to this question. Consider this following everyday script I have with my spouse:

ME.	What would you like for dinner tonight?
SPOUSE.	I don't know. I'm pretty much up for anything.
ME.	Would you like hamburgers tonight?
SPOUSE.	No, those don't really sound very good.
ME.	What about pizza?
SPOUSE.	No, I'm not in the mood for pizza.
ME.	How about some sandwiches?
SPOUSE.	No, I don't really feel like sandwiches.
ME.	What *would* you like to have?
SPOUSE.	I don't know...I'm pretty much up for anything...

How can we possibly answer the question of what we want *in life* when we can't even answer the question of what we want for dinner?

Sometimes, when we are trying to decide what we *want*, it is easier to start with what we *don't want*.

When I ask clients the question of what they want to do with their money, here are some of the answers I commonly hear:

ADVISOR. What do you want to do with your money?

CLIENT. Well...I know that I don't want to run out before I die...

And...I don't want to end up in a nursing home or be a burden to my spouse or my kids...

And...I don't want to leave so much money behind that I never enjoyed it...

And...I don't want to wait so long to enjoy it that my health goes downhill and I find myself wishing that I had done more when I was younger.

Before you know it, we start getting into the money worries:

CLIENT. My parents lived to the age of seventy, eighty, a hundred, or something like that; therefore, I probably only have X amount of years left to pull on this account. But...what if I live longer or shorter than that?

What about the taxes I'll owe? How does that factor in?

What if the stock market has another financial crisis like 2008? I don't have the time to wait to make up that kind of loss.

What if inflation skyrockets and then my money won't go very far at all? Can I even get my job back?

What if my medical costs go up and I can't afford to retire?

What if I die early? Does that mean I left too much on the table? I don't want to live like a pauper only to leave behind a bunch of money for my kids.

What does my spouse do if I die? I take care of everything, and he/she trusts me. Who helps him/her when I'm gone?

What will my kids do with my money if I die? I want them to do smart things with it. What if it destroys their lives like I've heard can happen to all those trust fund kids? I don't want to do that to them...And, if they blow it all on taxes and a new car, I think I'll roll over in my grave...

These questions and hundreds more show the worry that millions of Americans have about their finances. Here is the good news: these are the questions I have faced with thousands of clients over the past twenty years. If you were born in 1957, 1958, 1959, or 1960, then you are in luck. I have been helping your older siblings, older friends, and parents as they dealt with these questions for the past couple of decades. I am ready to help you. I will do the best I can to provide you with guidance on the pages ahead.

Regardless of *your* answer to the question "What do you want?" it all usually comes down to this:

> I don't want to run out. Oh, and by the way, I want as much as I can get. Oh, and by the way, if I die early, I want my family to get it. Oh, and by the way, if I live a long time, I don't really want to leave a bunch of it behind—my kids got me for a long time; they'll be happy with my house.

This last part isn't for everyone. Some of our clients want to leave a legacy. But many of our clients feel like they don't have enough money to leave a legacy, and they are focused on getting the maximum income for themselves. When it comes to your 401k, it is generally good to focus on maximum income for yourselves. This is because the Internal Revenue Service forces you to take money out of your 401k anyway once you reach seventy-three years old, and it's also good because we live in a progressive tax structure. That means that from a tax perspective your *traditional* 401k (or traditional IRA) is one of the *worst* assets to leave behind. (From a tax perspective, Roth IRAs and life insurance are much better assets to leave behind.)

When it comes to your traditional 401k and your traditional IRA, the best way to pay the least amount of taxes is to take many small distributions over a lot of years instead of a few big distributions that could bump you into higher tax brackets.

For example, let's imagine that you have $1 million in your 401k. You also have a decent pension and some Social Security benefits. You plan to live primarily on your pension and your Social Security benefits, and you think that you will just touch your 401k for those big purchases when they come up. In fact, your thoughts when you first retire are to take enough out of your 401k to pay off your house.

Now let's assume that you have a $250,000 mortgage on your home. You want to take out $250,000 from your 401k to pay off your house. Then maybe you can use the other $750,000 for other random expenses and live on your Social Security benefits and pension with a paid-off house.

What's wrong with this picture?

That's right—taxes. You see, to get $250,000 out of your 401k after taxes, you will need to take out somewhere between $350,000 and $450,000 just to receive a net amount of $250,000. Why? This is because the money in a *traditional 401k* is filled with *pretax* dollars. You had to *add* that $350,000 or $450,000 *on top* of your Social Security and pension income for that year. That will likely push your total *taxable income* into the highest tax brackets that exist in our country. You could be paying as much as 37 percent in federal income taxes plus whatever you owe in state income taxes.

So how much did that big withdrawal cost you? That probably cost you somewhere between $100,000 and $200,000 in federal and state income taxes. If you took those taxes from your 401k as well, then you only have $550,000 to $650,000 left in your 401k instead of the $750,000 you thought you would have. How long will that last now?

What would have happened if you'd taken that $450,000 out of your 401k over a long period of time? Let's consider the tax consequences of taking $45,000 per year out over ten years.

Now you are only adding $45,000 per year to your income. With that added on top of your Social Security benefits and your pension, you may find yourself earning somewhere between $75,000 and $125,000 of taxable income. There is a good chance that your *marginal tax rate* is now around 22 percent federally on the last dollar earned. (Your *effective tax rate* is likely even lower.) If we compare the difference between 22 percent and 37 percent, we are looking at a 15 percent disparity. Just to be clear: 15 percent of $450,000 is **$67,500!**

(The actual amount of money that you save by not paying interest on your home mortgage and/or the actual cost of income taxes for you are very important numbers for you to consider. I strongly recommend working with an accountant and a financial planner to determine the impact of taking a big withdrawal from your 401k before you actually take the money out. The bottom line: *there just might be a better way to take money out of your 401k than withdrawing it in a big lump sum that could put you in the highest tax brackets in our country.*)

So, like the title of our chapter, what now? Now that you realize big distributions can cost you a lot of money in taxes, then you have also realized you might pay less taxes overall if you take lots of little distributions over as many years as possible. If we agree with this conclusion, then what are the implications of this?

This means that you are going to be stuck with this 401k thing for most of your retirement. You have to manage this account through many years ahead. You have to figure out how you should invest it. You have to figure out how much you should take out each year.

This last realization speaks to the heart of the *best thing to do with your 401k*: take as much money out as you can, over as many years as possible, without running out.

HOW MUCH CAN I TAKE OUT WITHOUT RUNNING OUT?

Lots of very smart people have put a lot of brainpower, time, and computer energy into answering this question: How much can you take out without running out?

The answer to whether or not you will run out of money is of course dependent on a few variables: How aggressive/ volatile is your investment, how much will you take, and how long will you live?

Like any math equation, we can solve for one variable if we make assumptions for the others.

For example, when we see

$$2 + 2 = X$$

we know that X equals 4.

What if another number is replaced? For example, if we see

$$2 + X = 4$$

we know that X equals 2.

Now let's replace two numbers with letters. For example, let's consider this:

$$2 + X = Y$$

What does X equal? And Y?

There are lots of answers that are possible here. X could be 5, and then Y would be 7. X could be 3, and then Y would be 5. There are actually an infinite number of possibilities for X and Y.

This is the problem with answering the above question: *How Much Money Can I Take Out Without Running Out?* There are so many variables in that equation that there an infinite number of answers. *But, if we make assumptions for all the variables except one, then we can solve for that one missing variable.* (This is just like the equations above.)

This is what some really smart professors did when they put together a study known as "The Trinity Study" back in 1998.

Three professors from Trinity University made some assumptions to fill in the blanks in a formula and solve for the missing variable. They wanted to find out two things: (1) What was the highest *withdrawal percentage* that could be drawn from an investment portfolio without running out of money? (2) What was the *optimal allocation* between stocks and bonds for a person taking regular distributions from their investment? (These were both analyzed over thirty-year segments because a typical retirement experience was expected to last about thirty years. However, with medical technology nowadays and ever-increasing life expectancies, we may need to recalculate these numbers for an even longer retirement assumption in the future.)

Though the study is old, it is still quoted regularly by financial advisors, economists, and other experts even today. The results provided a lot of insight into the likely real-world answer to this question.

From this study came the following bottom-line rules of thumb: (1) A 75 percent stock / 25 percent bond allocation performed better than the other four allocations tested. (2) A 4 percent withdrawal rate was reasonably sustainable in the back-tested calculations.

Keep in mind that a lot of assumptions were made here that may not come to pass in the real world; in fact, several individuals have argued that many of the assumptions were wrong. And, as always, past performance does not necessarily indicate future results!

That being said, the most that could be pulled out of a portfolio over a thirty-year retirement experience (one of the assumptions worth reconsidering) is probably less than 6 percent per year (unless you are really lucky or have really amazing investment performance). The least amount you could pull out of an optimally allocated investment portfolio is probably more than 2 percent per year (unless your investments are poorly allocated or ultra conservative and/or we experience a whole new world makeover—like a nuclear war or something). Whether you think the amount you can draw is 4 percent per year, 3 percent per year, 5 percent per year, or some other number, you are going to have to *pick something.*

For our purposes of education, let's assume that a 4 percent withdrawal rate is sustainable. (Though, with people living much longer now and the market performance being very volatile in the twenty years since the study was performed, a 3 percent withdrawal rate is probably more prudent.)

With a 4 percent withdrawal rate this means that: if your 401k is worth $1 million, then you could probably draw out about $40,000 per year and not run out of money. (Caveat! Caveat! Disclosure! Disclosure! Must read above and understand this cannot be guaranteed!)

HOW DO I INVEST MY 401K?

Well, that's the conundrum, isn't it? How do we invest it?

Before we decide how to invest it, let's look at our investment experience so far.

We've probably just had our money in some kind of one-stop-shop asset allocation fund inside our 401k. These could be target-date funds aiming for a particular date of retirement, or they could be asset allocation funds based on our risk tolerance, like a moderate portfolio or something like that. Or, maybe we just put it into some stock index fund, such as one that mirrors the S&P 500.[2] Or, maybe it's still sitting in cash because we didn't want to risk it in the stock market again.

---

[2] Indexes are unmanaged, and investors cannot invest directly in an index. Unless otherwise noted, the performance of an index does not account for any fees, commissions, or other expenses that would be incurred. Returns do not include reinvested dividends. The Standard & Poor's 500 (S&P 500) is an unmanaged group of securities considered to be representative of the stock market in general. It is a market-value weighted index with each stock's weight in the index proportionate to its market value.

If you are already familiar with the asset allocation funds and index funds mentioned above, then you can likely skip the next section of this book. I have found, however, that many people don't have a clear understanding of what stocks, bonds, and mutual funds actually are. Moreover, many of the people I have met seem to make these concepts much more complicated than they need to be.

If you don't really understand what a stock is, what a bond is, or what mutual funds are, then this next section should make all of this stuff much clearer for you. If you have a pretty good idea, then this next section might make your understanding even clearer. If you are already an expert in investing and the basics of stocks, bonds, and mutual funds do not interest you, then please skip past the following gray-boxed section.

Stocks, Bonds, and Mutual Funds

What is a stock? What is a bond? What are mutual funds?

If you don't know the answer to these questions, relax; you are among the majority of people I have ever met. Furthermore, if you are brave enough to ask these questions and admit that you don't know, then you are in the minority of people humble enough to deserve the right answers.

These concepts are not complicated. It is just that many of the people who understand them do not teach them very clearly. If you read and understand the rest of the information in this box, then you will likely move yourself into the minority of people who "get it" when it comes to stocks, bonds, and mutual funds.

What is a stock?

A stock represents your *ownership* in a company. When you own a share of stock, you are a part owner of a company. For example, if you own a share of Disney stock, then you are a part owner of the Disney Corporation.

Every stock is purchased for two primary reasons: *change in value* or *dividends*.

Change in value: Let's say that you bought a share of stock for ten dollars. Then the company grew in value, and you sold it at eleven dollars per share. You just made 10 percent. Of course, if the company decreased in value to nine dollars per share and you sold it, then you just lost 10 percent.

Dividends: Every company is pretty much the same: *Revenue* comes in. *Expenses* go out. The difference between the two is called *profit*. When the company makes a profit, it can do two different things with it. It can either reinvest the profit into the company in an attempt to increase the value, or it can share the profit with the owners in the form of dividends. Dividends are just the amount of profit that a company decides to share with the owners.

What is a bond?

A bond represents a loan or a debt. When you buy a bond, it is as if the company (or government) that you are buying the bond from is *taking a loan out from you*.

Think about it. When you borrow money from someone, you have to pay the lender back the money you borrowed.

And, you pay interest because you were using the lender's money. When you buy a bond, the entity that you bought the bond from has to pay you back the principal (the amount you loaned the entity) and interest. (The interest is paid in the form of dividends on the bond.)

Individual bonds have two types of guarantees: guaranteed interest and guaranteed principal. You are guaranteed by the issuer of the bond to earn interest in the form of dividends, and your principal is guaranteed to be returned at the end of some time frame. That time frame is the time between now and the *maturity date*.

So how can you lose money when investing in bonds? If you loan your money to someone and they don't pay you back, then you have lost money. That is one risk that exists with bonds; it is called *default risk*. This is the risk that the issuer (government or corporation that borrowed money from you) doesn't pay you back. Another way to lose money in bonds is when you sell your bond to another investor for less money than you paid for it.

To understand this risk, it is best to go through an example. Imagine that you bought a bond that has a maturity date in twenty years paying an interest rate of 3 percent. This means that you will earn 3 percent interest each year for the next twenty years, and then you will get your money back (assuming that the issuer of the bond is still around and is ready to pay you back in twenty years). Now, let's imagine that five years go by. You have fifteen years left on your bond, but you have decided you want to sell it to someone else so you can use the principal (in other words, you want your money back earlier than twenty years).

You have to find a buyer who wants your bond. But how much is the buyer going to pay for your bond? That depends on the environment at that time. Has the issuer been dependable in paying back their debts? The dependability of the issuer in paying back their debts may have changed, and that could have an impact on the resale value of your bond. Also, how much could that buyer get as an interest rate if they buy a brand-new bond from the issuer? If interest rates have gone up (for example: imagine the issuer is now borrowing money at 5 percent instead of 3 percent), then why would anyone want your fifteen-year bond at 3 percent when they can get a brand-new one at a higher rate? You would have to sell your bond at a *discount* (or at a loss). On the other hand, if interest rates have gone down, then your bond might be more valuable than what the issuer is currently offering. That would mean you might be able to sell it at a *premium*.

This is the problem with investing in individual stocks and bonds. Your success in investing in them is 100 percent related to how you answer four questions: what to buy, when to buy, what to sell, and when to sell.

I do not profess to be an expert at answering these questions. Instead, we hire the experts to answer these questions for us. That is where a mutual fund comes in.

What is a mutual fund[3]?

A mutual fund is a conglomeration of people's money from all over the world. They all pool it together under the management of a specific person and/or group of people referred to as the portfolio manager(s). By combining money from many people, the fund typically has the ability to purchase a wider variety of stocks and/or bonds than any one person might be able to otherwise purchase individually with a smaller balance.

Mutual funds provide the ability for small investors to get more diversified with a smaller amount of money. They also provide the ability to hire a professional money manager and/or management company to make the above decisions for the client: what to buy, when to buy, what to sell, and when to sell.

These managers are required to invest the money within that fund according to the investment objective of the fund.

The investment objective is kind of like a general guideline for the portfolio manager that communicates the intentions of the manager and the purpose of the portfolio. The mutual fund also comes with rules that work kind of like handcuffs to prevent the portfolio manager(s) from investing outside the scope of the fund's purpose.

---

[3] Mutual funds are sold by prospectus. Please consider the investment objectives, risks, charges, and expenses carefully before investing in mutual funds. The prospectus, which contains this and other information about the investment company, can be obtained directly from the fund company or your financial professional. Be sure to read the prospectus carefully before deciding whether to invest.

For example, if you invest in a US large-cap growth fund, then the manager will be investing in domestic companies (US) that are also larger companies (large cap) with a *growth* philosophy. You would not expect to find international companies, small companies, and/or bonds in this portfolio. And if the manager tried to buy things that were outside the scope of the investment objective (break their handcuffs), then they would be prevented from doing so by the mutual fund company they work with.

To track the portion of each fund that belongs to each investor, the mutual fund issues *shares* just like a company issues shares of stock. These shares are priced daily at the close of the stock market. The price per share of a mutual fund is quoted as *NAV* (net asset value). You can find this price and performance history by searching on the internet for the *ticker symbol* of the mutual fund.[4]

Because of the convenience of mutual funds (the ability to invest in a diversified, professionally managed portfolio with a relatively small amount of money), they have become the predominant way of investing inside 401k accounts. There is a good chance that if you have a 401k, then you are already investing in mutual funds.

There are thousands of different mutual funds and thousands of different portfolio managers and management styles.

---

[4] A ticker symbol is a code that allows people to quickly search for prices of stocks, mutual funds, and other types of securities that trade on a stock exchange. As another side point, there are three main stock exchanges (places to trade or buy and sell stocks and other securities) in the Unites States: the New York Stock Exchange, the American Stock Exchange, and the NASDAQ.

Every fund takes a slightly different approach to investing, but most financial advisors who work with them group these funds into certain categories to better analyze their performance and help their clients choose which funds they might want to use in their portfolio.

Typically, these funds are grouped based on the type of securities they invest in, the size of the securities they invest in, the location of the securities they invest in, and the general management philosophy of the manager(s). The types could be *stocks, bonds,* or *other securities.* The size is typically a reference to help subcategorize the stock positions referring to *large cap, midcap, small cap,* and *microcap.* The location is typically categorized by companies that are *domestic, international developed,* or *international emerging markets.* Finally, the philosophy is typically either *growth* or *value.* There are also *managed funds* and *index funds.*

One can easily see how analyzing these various funds, choosing an allocation, choosing an investment strategy, and monitoring the ongoing performance can be a daunting task. Nevertheless, a significant portion of your money is most likely invested in mutual funds right now within your 401k. *Making sure that you are in the right funds for you is ultimately your responsibility. Making sure that you do the right thing with your money as you near and enter retirement is also your responsibility.*

I hope that this book helps you find more clarity as you shoulder these responsibilities.

There are all kinds of places that your money could be invested right now, but where do you want to invest it for the next thirty years? (That's right, by the way. Your retirement could easily be thirty years long or even longer.)

You are not in the same life situation in retirement as you were during your working years.

If the market value goes down, you can't simply wait to touch the money. You will need an income stream to supplement your Social Security income. (Social Security is *not* designed to be the only source of retirement income.)

If the market goes down while you are withdrawing an income stream from your 401k, then you will be forced to sell your investments when the value of your securities is low.

That's not good. But like we said, you can't wait to touch the money. You need the income to live on in retirement. So what do you do?

You *must* take a new approach to investing!

You have just finished your *accumulation* years, the period of time when you accumulated your wealth. Your attitude during that time was (or should have been) different than in retirement. You could take more risk in those years. You had time to recover. You could wait to touch your money.

Now, you are about to enter your *distribution* years. This is the period of time where you will be taking distributions from your accounts. This is a very different time in your life, and it should require a very different investment strategy.[5]

One of the biggest mistakes that financial advisors see is that clients change their phase of life (move into the distribution phase), but they *don't* change their investment strategy.

Why is this such a big deal?

Because there was this little friend that helped your 401k during your accumulation years. Its name was *dollar cost averaging.* Unfortunately, that same little friend who helped you during all those years will hurt you during the distribution phase of your life. There is a thing known as *reverse dollar cost averaging,* and it creates a whole new type of risk called *sequence of return risk.* And this thing is something that you *must* learn about, or it will take a huge bite out of your 401k in retirement.

So what is dollar cost averaging[6]?

---

[5] In an ideal world, you haven't just flipped a switch between *accumulation* and *distribution.* Ideally, you have included an in-between phase for at least a few years we refer to as *preservation.* This is the period of time when you preserve your assets against loss shortly before you change your strategy for distribution.

This preservation phase can last anywhere from a few years to more than a decade. It just depends on your appetite for risk. There is no right or wrong answer to how long you should be in the preservation phase.

However, if you are already in your late fifties or early sixties, you should probably be making this decision quickly or have already made this decision by now.

[6] Dollar cost averaging may help reduce per share cost through continuous investment in securities regardless of fluctuating prices but does not guarantee profitability, nor can it protect from loss in a declining market. The investor should consider his/her ability to continue investing though periods of low price levels.

Dollar cost averaging is what happens when you put *fixed dollar amounts* into an investment account over a regular period of time. (Kind of like you did with your 401k, right?)

Imagine that you put $100 per month into your 401k. Every month $100 goes in, and at the end of the year you have invested $1,200.

Now, imagine that every month you purchased shares of your investment with that $100. Take a look at the following chart:

CHART 1

	January	February	March	April	May	June	July
Invested	$100.00	$100.00	$100.00	$100.00	$100.00	$100.00	$100.00
Price Per Share	$5.00	$5.00	$5.00	$5.00	$5.00	$5.00	$5.00
Number of Shares Purchased	20.00	20.00	20.00	20.00	20.00	20.00	20.00

August	September	October	November	December	
$100.00	$100.00	$100.00	$100.00	$100.00	$1,200.00 TOTAL INVESTED
$5.00	$5.00	$5.00	$5.00	$5.00	
20.00	20.00	20.00	20.00	20.00	240.00 SHARES PURCHASED

x $5.00   CURRENT PRICE PER SHARE
$1,200.00   CURRENT VALUE

When the price per share is the same every single month, we purchase the same number of shares with each contribution. Then, at the end of the year, the value of the account is equal to your contributions ($1,200). The account hasn't grown at all.

But in the real world most investments change in value every day! So a real-life chart would look more like this:

CHART 2

	January	February	March	April	May	June	July
Invested	$100.00	$100.00	$100.00	$100.00	$100.00	$100.00	$100.00
Price Per Share	$5.00	$4.00	$6.00	$8.00	$3.00	$4.00	$5.00
Number of Shares Purchased	20.00	25.00	16.67	12.50	33.33	25.00	20.00

August	September	October	November	December		
$100.00	$100.00	$100.00	$100.00	$100.00	$ 1,200.00	TOTAL INVESTED
$4.00	$3.00	$6.00	$7.00	$5.00		
25.00	33.33	16.67	14.29	20.00		261.79 SHARES PURCHASED

x $5.00 CURRENT PRICE PER SHARE

$ 1,308.93 CURRENT VALUE

$108.93 EXTRA MONEY LOST FROM REVERSE DOLLAR COST AVERAGING

As you can see in the chart above, the real world has you purchasing a very different number of shares each month. But let's take a look at what else happened.

Every time you put a fixed amount of money *into* your account, you purchased *more shares* when the price per share was *lower* and *fewer shares* when the price per share was *higher*. Have you ever heard of "buy low and sell high"? By putting a similar amount of money into your 401k *each and every month,* you have systematically been *buying low* more often than you bought high. This has resulted in you purchasing more shares at an average price per share that is *lower* than the actual *average price.*

Average price = 5

Average price per share = $4.58

This is the remarkable benefit of dollar cost averaging.

You gained an extra $108.93 in value from the $1,200 invested in this example!

Unfortunately, the "evil twin" (as one of my colleagues refers to this) of dollar cost averaging is *reverse dollar cost averaging* which creates *sequence of return risk.*

Look at what happens in the same example as above when we start *withdrawing* $100 per month:

CHART 3

	January	February	March	April	May	June	July
Withdrawn	$100.00	$100.00	$100.00	$100.00	$100.00	$100.00	$100.00
Price Per Share	$5.00	$4.00	$6.00	$8.00	$3.00	$4.00	$5.00
Number of Shares Sold	20.00	25.00	16.67	12.50	33.33	25.00	20.00

August	September	October	November	December		
$100.00	$100.00	$100.00	$100.00	$100.00	$1,200.00	TOTAL RECEIVED
$4.00	$3.00	$6.00	$7.00	$5.00		
25.00	33.33	16.67	14.29	20.00	261.79	SHARES SOLD

x $5.00 CURRENT PRICE PER SHARE

$1,308.93 CURRENT VALUE IF SHARES WEREN'T SOLD

$108.93 EXTRA MONEY LOST FROM REVERSE DOLLAR COST AVERAGING

Because you sold shares to produce a level amount of income, more shares needed to be sold when the price of the investment was *lower*, and fewer shares needed to be sold when the price of the shares was *higher*. *All the **gains** experienced by the dollar cost averaging investor become **losses** experienced by the reverse dollar cost averaging withdrawer!*

This means that if you retire right before a market decline, then reverse dollar cost averaging *out* of your investment portfolio can rapidly erode your account balance. An unlucky sequence of returns has the potential to decimate your retirement nest egg. So, what does this mean? It means that you *must* change your investment strategy once you are in the distribution phase of life.

Now that we understand a little bit about why we need to change our strategy, it is time to determine how we change the strategy and what we invest our money in.

One of our most popular strategies for optimizing your investment portfolio is to use a bucket approach to investing. This helps us avoid the losses from your enemy—reverse-dollar cost averaging. Whether or not you use an annuity, using this approach is an excellent way to start thinking differently about how to invest your money during your *distribution* phase.

The bucket strategy is simple. We think about the money that you want to touch right away (in zero to five years), and we invest that very conservatively. (This way the share price doesn't go up and down so much on an account that we are withdrawing from. We decrease our risk of losses due to reverse dollar cost averaging. Then we invest with a little more risk using the money you want to touch in years five through ten. Then the money that you don't plan to touch for more than ten years can be invested with even more risk.

My good friend Jason Smith has an excellent book that can provide a lot more detail on this strategy. It is called *The Bucket Plan*, and it can be purchased on Amazon or at many bookstores near you.

But when all is said and done, you have to pick an investment to put your money in.

With that in mind, you can only pick one of two types of accounts: accounts *with guarantees* and accounts *without guarantees*[7].

---

[7] Guarantees provided are based on the claims-paying ability of the issuing company.

CHAPTER

HOW DOES THE NON-GUARANTEED APPROACH WORK?

The non-guaranteed approach is pretty typical among many investment firms and financial advisory practices today. In general, the idea is this: invest your money in some combination of stocks, bonds, mutual funds, and/or cash. Invest with the right amount of risk (based on your personal tolerance of fluctuations in value). Try the best you can to get a decent rate of return. Balance the account with diversification[8] to create more stable results. And, finally, try to draw out a reasonable amount each year.

"Reasonable," of course, is a moving target.

In a good year, you might be inclined to pull out extra. In a bad year, you will probably feel uncomfortable touching your account, so you will pull out less. Unfortunately, this leads to

---

[8] Diversification does not guarantee a profit or protect against a loss in a declining market. It is a method used to help manage investment risk.

fluctuating income, and fluctuating income can be a very hard thing to tolerate when you are retired and trying to live on limited means or a fixed budget.

With the bucket approach you can smooth out your income. Start with a fixed percentage that you would like to draw out of your retirement account. Make a conscious choice as to how much this will be. If you think 5 percent is sustainable or you have a shorter life expectancy, then you might choose 5 percent. If you think you might live a long time, or you are conservative and very worried about running out of money, you might choose 2 percent or 3 percent.

After you pick your percentage, you set up your accounts to distribute this amount of money for yourself over the years ahead.

For example: Let's imagine that you have $1 million set aside for retirement in your 401k. You feel comfortable at a 4 percent withdrawal percentage. You plan to pull out 4 percent of the $1 million per year or $40,000 per year.

Congratulations! You have just started the financial planning process. You drew a line in the sand and said, "I feel good about pulling out $40,000 per year." Now what?

Next you decide how much money you want in bucket number one. Let's say that you want five years of income in that bucket. So you set aside about $40,000 X 5 years (or $200,000).

Then, because you know that you will be drawing from that bucket for the next five years as an income source, you invest that *very conservatively*. (You might even put this portion of your money in a savings account or money market. This all depends on *your* risk tolerance.)

Next, you set aside enough to cover your income in years six through ten. You might want to give yourself a raise due to inflation, so you anticipate that you will need $45,000 or even $50,000 per year at that time.[9]

If we assume that we need about $50,000 X 5 years (years six through ten), then we need about $250,000 for bucket number two. We can invest bucket number two into something designed to give you a little interest based on your risk tolerance and your comfort with various investments. If we assume that the investments in bucket two earn you 3 percent interest on average per year (not a guaranteed rate of return by any means), then we can invest a little more than $215,000 right now and have it worth about $250,000 in five years.[10]

Now you have allocated $415,000 of your $1 million retirement account ($200,000 to cover income for the first five years and $215,000 to cover income for years six to ten). So what do you do with the remaining $585,000?

You can invest it with the knowledge that you don't *plan to touch it* for the next ten years!

---

[9] The income target of $45,000 assumes a 2.36 percent rate of inflation; $50,000 assumes a 4.47 percent rate of inflation. We, of course, have no idea what actual inflation will be like over the next five years, so we just have to guess.

[10] The higher the rate of return, the less money you need to set aside for this income. The lower the rate of return (0 percent for example), the more you need to put into bucket number two to cover the $250,000 of income for years six to ten.

This usually leaves you feeling comfortable taking a bit more risk with bucket number three. If you take more risk, then you can seek out a higher rate of return. (Of course, you should not take any more risk than you feel comfortable taking.) In the end, you hope that the $585,000 in bucket number three grows enough over the next ten years to generate enough money to keep drawing from it while refilling your bucket number one and bucket number two as you get closer to emptying these buckets over the years ahead.[11]

In general, this strategy accomplishes two things that help tremendously in your retirement. (1) You have decreased the impact from the evil twin of dollar cost averaging—*reverse dollar cost averaging*. (2) By separating your buckets, you will usually be able to get a higher *average overall* rate of return than you would have received if you simply put all your investments in one account with the belief that you might touch *all of it* at any given moment now that you are retired.

Whether you use stocks, bonds, mutual funds, ETFs, money markets, REITs, alternative investments, gold coins, savings accounts, CDs, or any other kind of investment is *up to you*. We recommend working with a financial professional to help you design this kind of plan and partner with the right investment managers to get the best rate of return you can earn with your risk tolerance.

As we evaluate this strategy, we can see where there are still a lot of *what-ifs* remaining.

---

[11] The ideal timing of refilling buckets along the way and the adjustment of your investments to your risk tolerance are complicated. We highly recommend working with an experienced financial advisor throughout this process to ensure you are getting the best returns you can earn for the amount of risk you are willing to take.

What if I don't get that 3 percent rate of return on bucket number two? What if I am too risky with my bucket number three and I lose too much? What if $40,000 (4 percent) was too high of a withdrawal percentage, and I live longer than I thought? What if I leave too much money behind, and I could have really enjoyed retirement with a lot more?

These are questions that all stem from one primary fear: *I don't want to run out of money.* These questions need to be answered in either the guaranteed or the non-guaranteed approach. However, the guaranteed approach does provide reassurance and certainty to many of these questions that the non-guaranteed approach simply cannot provide.

HOW DOES THE GUARANTEED APPROACH WORK?

How does it work? Well, it guarantees you that you *won't run out of money.*

How does it do that? Well, you pay an insurance company to protect you in the event that you run out of money.

How does an insurance company do that? Well, they do it by providing you with an annuity.[12]

Here is the basic annuity strategy: you put a portion of your 401k money into an annuity contract. Then the insurance company that issues you the annuity contract guarantees you

---

[12] But what if you don't know if you want to use an annuity? I totally get it, but put that thought on a shelf for a moment while you learn about how this works. You can always decide to go back and use the non-guaranteed approach. Remember there is no wrong answer here. You have earned the money in your 401k. It is up to you to decide what you want to do with it. I just recommend learning about all the options and making an informed choice. If you are interested in learning about the guaranteed approach, then keep on reading.

that you can take out a certain amount of money per year for a certain period of time. (The amount of money you can take is based on three factors: your age, the amount of money you invest in the annuity, and the rules of your annuity contract.)

Annuities[13] have been around for hundreds of years. The general definition of an annuity is a stream of income that is guaranteed to last for a specific period of time. Most of the types of annuities that people work with today *must* provide a distribution option that produces a guaranteed income

---

[13] Fixed annuities are long-term insurance contracts, and there is a surrender charge imposed, generally during the first five to seven years that you own the annuity contract. Withdrawals prior to age fifty-nine and a half may result in a 10 percent IRS tax penalty in addition to any ordinary income tax. Any guarantees of the annuity are backed by the financial strength of the underlying insurance company.

Indexed annuities are insurance contracts that, depending on the contract, may offer a guaranteed annual interest rate and some participation in growth, if any, of a stock market index. Such contracts have substantial variations in terms, costs of guarantees, and features and may cap participation or returns in significant ways. Any guarantees offered are backed by the financial strength of the insurance company. Surrender charges apply if the annuity is not held to the end of the term. Withdrawals are taxed as ordinary income and subject to a 10 percent federal tax penalty if taken prior to age fifty-nine and a half. Investors are cautioned to carefully review an indexed annuity for its features, costs, and risks as well as how the variables are calculated.

Please consider the investment objectives, risks, charges, and expenses carefully before investing in variable annuities. The prospectus, which contains this and other information about the variable annuity contract and the underlying investment options, can be obtained from the insurance company or your financial professional. Be sure to read the prospectus carefully before deciding whether to invest.

The investment return and principal value of the variable annuity investment options are not guaranteed. Variable annuity subaccounts fluctuate with changes in market conditions. The principal may be worth more or less than the original amount invested when the annuity is surrendered.

stream that lasts as long as you live. That's right—they have to pay you a certain amount of money on a regular basis, and they have to guarantee you that you can't outlive it.

These are the only accounts that can provide you the certainty that your income will never stop coming in as long as you are breathing.

How much should you put in? What happens to the money if you die? Which type should you use?

These questions are addressed in the chapters ahead. But let's start by answering the question of why some people say they hate annuities.

WHY DO SOME PEOPLE SAY THEY HATE ANNUITIES?

There are a few answers to this question, and we will explore and explain the reasons behind each of them. The quick answers in bullet form, however, are as follows:

- Many people don't like paying for insurance of any sort.
- Many older types of annuities used to be more expensive, more restrictive, and less advantageous.
- Many previous buyers of annuities didn't understand what they were buying (possibly due to poor explanation or misinformation, but also possibly due to clients forgetting what they bought—annuities are an insurance contract, and they can be complicated).

Let's start with some insights into why people don't like paying for insurance.

You see, whenever you have a risk that you don't want to have, you have two choices: either avoid the activity or situation that has risk or pay for someone else to take the risk for you.

Avoiding the activity is easier with some things and harder with others. For example, you can avoid the risk of being eaten by a shark by not swimming in the ocean. Pretty easy to avoid, right? On the other hand, you can also avoid the risk of your house burning down by not living in a house. That one is a bit harder. Not living in a house (or somewhere with walls and a roof) isn't really something most of us are willing to do just to avoid the risk of a house fire. We all want to live somewhere, but the cost of our house burning down would be devastating to the financial plan of most people.

So how do we avoid the risk of our house burning down without being homeless? The answer: we pay an insurance company to take the risk for us. That's what homeowner's insurance is.

It's hard to imagine having a home without homeowners' insurance or having a car with no car insurance. Or imagine what life would be like without health insurance, disability insurance, or life insurance. Horribly expensive negative situations can arise in these areas, and we rely on insurance companies to help us deal with catastrophic circumstances.

Most people who are healthy complain about paying for their health insurance. People who never have a car accident often hate paying for their car insurance. People whose houses don't burn down generally don't like paying for homeowners' insurance. Insurance isn't there for the majority of people who don't use it; it is there to help the few people who do use it.

Have you ever known a person who had their house burn down? Do you think they felt like they had too much homeowner's insurance? Or, have you ever known a really sick person who thought they had too much health insurance? Or have you ever met a widow or widower who thought his/her spouse had too much life insurance?

So what do we do about the risk of running out of money before we die? Who offers 'live too long' insurance? Who will take away the risk for us that we might run out of money?

That is what annuities were created to do.

So what about the other two reasons why people say they hate annuities?

Unfortunately, like most histories, the evolution of the annuity insurance contract is filled with missteps, misunderstandings, adjustments, improvements, modifications, bankruptcies, legal restrictions, and general failures of clear communication. This history has led to more regulation, frustration, and general anti-annuity sentiment by a lot of individuals. Many of these individuals stopped learning about annuities long ago. Therefore, many people have failed to observe the significant improvements that have come to pass in the annuity world. These people are often preaching antiquated opinions that are no longer accurate, and they have failed to keep up on the continued education necessary to fully grasp the concept of the modern-day annuity contract.

You will learn more than many of these pundits in the next section as you observe the evolution of annuities.

The Evolution of Annuities

There is more to the passionate anti-annuity sentiment than simply not wanting to pay for the costs of insurance.

To understand the animosity against annuities, we have to explore their history.

The annuity of one hundred years ago is very different from the annuities of today.

When the nonqualified annuity was originally created in the United States, it was made for a few wealthy individuals.

Story 1

Imagine that you are a successful entrepreneur in the early 1900s. Many of your friends are employees of various companies, and their retirement is taken care of. They have pensions.

You, on the other hand, have a decent amount of money, but without a pension, you are worried that you might live too long and run out. So you decide that you would like to shift that risk to an insurance company by buying your own pension.

You walk into the insurance company with the equivalent in today's dollars of $1 million. You are now sixty years old, and you believe that you have a shot of living past one hundred. The insurance company decides to make a deal with you. If you give them the $1 million, then they will guarantee to pay you an income *immediately* of $80,000 per year for the rest of your life. But if you die early, they get to keep all the rest of the money.

You do the math and believe that you will live past the break-even point (age seventy-two and a half is when you would have received total income payments that are equal to your original $1 million invested). So you buy the annuity.

This is the original version of an annuity. It is basically a pension plan that is purchased by an individual. You hope that you live a long time and collect $80,000 per year for the next forty-plus years (giving you $3.2 million or more in this example). The insurance company hopes that you pass away soon so that they get to keep the unused remainder of your $1 million.

This worked for a small group of wealthy investors who really wanted protection against living too long and who wanted a guaranteed income stream that they could count on. It was used as a conservative part of an overall asset investment strategy, and it was not nearly as common among the masses as the annuities of today are.

(This kind of annuity still exists today. We call it a single premium immediate annuity or a SPIA. It can be a good way to turn a lump sum of money into a payout over a period of years. They can be guaranteed to pay out for life or even over a specific number of years whether you are alive or not. These are most often used by attorneys creating lifetime income streams, lottery winners choosing payout options over several years, and pension plan participants who forfeit the lump sum benefit in return for a longer payout of an income stream. It can be used to help prevent newly wealthy individuals from overspending and running out of money. It can also be used to provide income for a specific period of time in a dependable way. In general, these types of annuities are very rarely used with 401k plans because newer annuities can provide similar guaranteed lifetime income benefits without immediately giving up the remaining money in your account when you die.)

Story 2

Now imagine that you are a younger friend of our wealthy entrepreneur in Story 1. It's still the early 1900s, but you are only thirty-five years old. Like your friend, you also believe that you will live a long time, and you want to put money aside to create a pension you can draw on when you retire at sixty years old.

You put your money into an annuity as well, but you *defer* receiving your income until a later date (like when you reach sixty years old).

You put your money into this annuity, and because you aren't planning to touch it for another twenty-five years, you get to earn interest on the money while you wait to take it out. What's more is that the IRS knows that you are setting this aside for retirement purposes, so they make a deal with you too. They agree to *not* tax you on your earnings until you take the money out later on down the road.[14] (This kind of tax benefit is what we call *tax-deferred growth*. The 401k's of today also receive this benefit—that's why you don't have to pay taxes on your 401k earnings during your *accumulation* phase.)

---

[14] Of course, to get this benefit, the IRS forces you to follow through with the annuitization process or wait until you are fifty-nine and a half years old to touch the money. If you try to randomly withdraw this money before reaching the age of fifty-nine and a half, you will find yourself facing normal income taxes on the earnings *and* a 10 percent penalty tax, which is quite similar to the 401k plans you're used to.

You do the math, and you realize that you can put some money away for later. Because you get tax-deferred growth, you believe that this annuity will help you amass a lot more money than a traditional investment that you might have to otherwise pay taxes on over the next twenty-five years. And since you want to set up a pension for yourself anyway, you feel good about turning the lump sum into a pension-like payout for life when you hit sixty years old or some other time down the road.

When you reach sixty years old and are ready to start taking the pension payout, you call the insurance company and instruct them to *annuitize* your contract. This means that you have officially left the *accumulation* phase and entered the *annuitization* phase. This also means that you have given up your rights to the balance inside your annuity in return for the pension-like payout. (The amount of that payout will be based on the value of the account when you annuitize it, your age, the current interest rate environment, and the rules of your annuity contract.)

We understand what happens if you die *after* you have annuitized the contract: the insurance company gets to keep whatever is left of your balance. But what happens if you pass away *before* you annuitized your contract, when you are still in the accumulation phase?

If you pass away before you have annuitized your investment, then your heirs get to receive the balance of your annuity contract. They get to take it out in a variety of ways that have differing income tax consequences, but they haven't missed out on receiving all the money you set aside for yourself in retirement. It's still there until you choose to annuitize the contract.

(This kind of annuity also still exists today. In fact, this above strategy can be done with every kind of annuity that exists other than a SPIA. Fortunately, the contracts of today are rarely annuitized. You will understand that more as we progress through the evolution of annuities in the stories ahead.)

Story 3

Imagine that you are still our same successful entrepreneur in Story 2. You are thirty-five years old, and you are investing a bunch of money each and every year into this annuity contract to create a pension for yourself down the road.

You are single in this story. You don't have any children or a spouse, so you aren't worried about leaving any money behind. Your goal is to get the highest guaranteed income for as long as you live starting at age sixty.

But at forty years old, your life changes. You meet your spouse and fall in love.

When you get to sixty years old, you've changed your mind. You don't want to give up the money for a pension just for you.

Don't worry. Everything will be fine. You can have a calculation done that will protect *you and your spouse*. You can get a guaranteed payout from the insurance company that will pay an income stream to either of you as long as either of you is alive.

Of course, the odds that at least one of you will be alive in the years ahead are better than the odds that just you will be alive. Therefore, the insurance company gets to adjust the calculation when you annuitize. They determine that you will receive *less* than they promised before because you are protecting *two people*, and the odds that you will both die soon are lower than the odds that you alone might die early.

This type of annuitization is available on all annuity contracts of the past and today. This is called a *joint-and-survivor annuitization* option. It is a good way to protect two people with a guaranteed income stream. But when you both pass away, the remainder still gets kept by the insurance company.

Can you start to imagine why there are some annuitization stories that might result in angry people?

What if you were the children of the above couple in the story? You knew that your parents had millions of dollars in accounts. They lived a luxurious life and spent ridiculous amounts of money as they lived on the income from their annuities and maybe some Social Security benefits. When they both died, you thought there would be a huge inheritance just waiting for you.

You find out that all the money was spent over your parents' lifetimes. Maybe they left you some personal belongings and maybe a house, but the millions that you had been counting on were gone.

It doesn't matter that your parents may have put in $500,000 over their lifetime and received millions while they were alive. You missed out on your inheritance. You are angry. You decided to tell the media and your attorney about how horrible this annuity thing was. Your parents have passed away in this story. They aren't there to tell you (or the media or your attorney) about how wonderful this annuity was *for them.*

What if the story wasn't so generous for your parents? What if they passed away in a car accident only a month or two after they had annuitized?

Many of us know of stories where a friend or an acquaintance worked their whole life for a pension. They retired, and then they died shortly afterward. They hardly collected any of their pension, and their heirs didn't get anything from the pension they were now unable to collect.

These are the same kinds of stories that have brought a negative spotlight to annuities. This is especially aggravated if the insurance agent who provided the annuity to the parents was unclear or intentionally dishonest about the fact that the children or other heirs wouldn't get to receive any of the annuity proceeds after it was annuitized. Of course, by the time the children are disappointingly protesting, the parents are often not around to exonerate the honest agents or incriminate the dishonest ones.

(The vast majority of insurance professionals I have come to know over the decades have been some of the most selfless, caring, and giving individuals I have ever met. I firmly believe that a few bad apples combined with disappointed heirs, zealous media representatives, and hungry attorneys have drastically exaggerated the negative opinion surrounding annuities. However, there are still more negative surprises to come in the annuity evolution story.)

Story 4

You are still our successful tycoon from story 3. You are married, you have kids, and you do not want to forfeit the millions of dollars that you accumulated in your annuity contract at sixty years old. You are no longer worried about you and your spouse outliving your money. You have enough money from other sources, and you don't want to follow through with the annuitization process. What do you do?

Well, you *don't have to annuitize* that contract. You can remain in the *accumulation* phase and postpone annuitization to a much later age.[15] But what if you still want to get at some of the money while you're alive? Okay, no problem. The insurance company will allow you to take *withdrawals during the accumulation phase.*

You haven't annuitized the contract, so you haven't given up the principal. Now you can take withdrawals out of your account and treat it like most other investment accounts that you have. Of course, if you are under fifty-nine and a half years old, then the IRS wants to penalize you with a 10 percent penalty tax for touching the account too early. But if you draw the money out after age fifty-nine and a half, then you just have to pay income taxes on the earnings. (Of course, the earnings must all *come out first* and be taxed. Then your after-tax principal is the last to come out of the contract tax-free. This tax treatment is known as *last in first out* or *LIFO*. It is very rare to have after-tax money in a traditional 401k plan.

---

[15] Most annuity contracts of today let you postpone annuitization until age ninety or later. If you reach the maximum age, then you can also usually choose a period-certain annuitization option that guarantees your heirs receive the payout even if you pass away during the payout period.

Therefore, everything that comes out of the 401k plan is usually subject to income taxes.)

These four stories illustrate how annuities were used when they were first created. As you can see, the typical user of these types of contracts was a wealthy individual who didn't already have a pension. They wanted tax-deferred growth in the accumulation phase, and they wanted a guaranteed pension-like payout when they retired.

The insurance companies who created and sold these contracts made sure that they calculated the pension-like payouts in a reasonable way so that they would collect enough money to cover the amounts that they had to pay out and still leave enough of a difference to create a reasonable profit. As for the contracts that were in the accumulation phase, the insurance companies were able to charge a significant annual fee because of the favorable tax treatment.

It didn't cost the insurance company anything to have the benefits of tax-deferred growth on their annuity contracts, and it saved the wealthy client lots of tax dollars. So the insurance company felt that it was fair to charge high percentages as an annual fee to use these types of investments.

This is pretty much how annuities were used until the late 1970s.

What happened next?

In 1978 the 401k was born.

You may or may not remember the beginnings of 401k's, but it is likely that you missed an interesting tax code that came out right around the same time—the 403b.

This tax code created an account just like 401k's, but it was for employees of nonprofit organizations. These employees are our everyday heroes: teachers, firefighters, police officers, and other governmental employees.

What was different about the 403b tax code and the 401k tax code is that 403b plans *could only be funded with annuities*. That's right. Our heroes didn't have the ability to use the more common mutual funds that were available in 401k plans. They had to use annuity contracts. Why? Simply put, insurance companies managed to lobby for this monopoly. They probably used the argument that pensions were the traditional retirement for these nonprofit employees, and they would therefore want their 403b assets to have the pension option that annuities provided. While variable annuities did have the ability to invest in mutual fund–like subaccounts, the internal expenses on these contracts were *much higher* than traditional mutual fund investments.

This had significant ramifications.

Remember that these 403b accounts were being funded with the older, more expensive annuity contracts. In addition to these higher expenses, they also had very long surrender charges (often ten to twenty years in length). These fees would penalize the owner if they took money out or transferred it away from the annuity prematurely. Furthermore, many of these teachers, firefighters, and police officers did not realize that their 403b-annuity contract was more expensive than their friend's 401k plan that was funded with the lower-cost mutual funds. (Of course, the pension option of the annuities and other features—like an account that pays fixed, CD-like interest rates—aren't available by using mutual funds in the 401k plan, but many people forget that now.)

What happened next? The stock market did pretty great through the '80s. Account balances in 401k's were climbing rapidly. Unfortunately, our public employees' 403b accounts were not experiencing growth as fast as their friends in the private sector. They talked to each other. Some people figured out that they weren't making as much interest in variable annuities due to the higher expenses or in fixed annuities because they weren't in the stock market. These public employees wanted to use mutual funds, but they couldn't because of the regulations. So they complained.

The regulations got changed in the early 1990s, and the 403b tax code was amended to include provision 403b(7). Now public employees could use mutual funds in their 403b accounts.

As more and more of the new public employees chose not to use annuities and transferred their money into lower-cost mutual fund accounts, the insurance companies realized that they had to make changes. They decided to decrease their costs and shorten their surrender charges[16] to be more competitive.

This brings us to the late '90s. Annuities had a bit of a bad rep because of the disappointed public employees who had paid too much in their variable annuity 403b accounts, and media stories of disappointed beneficiaries, forgetful elderly clients,

---

[16] Reminder: surrender charges are penalties that the insurance companies charge customers when they move their money away from the insurance companies earlier than they agreed to in the contract.

and dishonest insurance sales people further clouded the reputation of annuities. However, in spite of this challenging image, most of the annuities being placed were doing exactly what they were designed to do: providing high-income distribution amounts that the owners were guaranteed not to outlive.

Around this time, however, insurance companies discovered yet another competitive advantage over mutual funds. *They could provide insurance that protected their clients' income without giving up the money when they die!*

A couple of insurance companies created an innovation on their annuity contract that could guarantee clients their money back even if the stock market went down. (They did this by restricting the access to the account to 7 percent or less of the original invested amount per year, but cumulatively contract owners were guaranteed to get all their money back or more regardless of what happened to their investments in the stock market.) In addition, this kind of guarantee was available during the *accumulation phase* of the annuity contract, so the contract owner *didn't have to annuitize.* (This meant investors didn't have to give up the money that was left in the account if they died before getting it all out.) What was even better was that the insurance companies priced this extra guarantee at what they expected their actual costs to be. (They didn't build in a profit margin for this added feature; they just wanted to attract clients to invest with them, because they knew that they would make enough profit from the basic investor using *their* annuity instead of a competitor's.)

This concept revolutionized annuities. Sadly, however, many investors and advisors were too jaded about the history of annuities to notice.

In spite of the anti-annuity sentiment, annuities started to attract the attention of more and more investors. There was finally a way to invest in the stock market[17] and be guaranteed not to lose!

These couple of innovating insurance companies gained so much market share from the other annuity providers that the other annuity competitors hopped on the bandwagon and created their own guarantees. Because investors could receive these guaranteed income benefits while they were alive, these guarantees became referred to in the industry as *living benefits*.

What happened next was what we affectionately refer to as the Cold War of Living Benefits.

Every insurance company started one-upping the other insurance companies. They offered better and better benefits at lower and lower costs. We saw guarantees at the peak of this "cold war" that offered as high as 6 percent guaranteed withdrawals per year for life with a guaranteed insurance number that would grow at 6 percent per year or whatever growth rate the investments grew at—*whichever was greater!*

We worked hard to make sure that our clients had the best guarantees that we could find as the landscape of guarantees rapidly changed. Many of our clients intentionally chose the

---

[17] Reminder: variable annuities allowed for mutual fund-like subaccounts that included stocks and bonds with similar allocations and objectives to mutual funds.

shortest surrender charge periods possible on these contracts (typically three or four years in the early 2000s) so that they could switch to a different (potentially better) contract at the end of their surrender charge if the contracts continued to get better.

Then 2008 happened. The financial crisis changed the way that the insurance companies were looking at the risk they were taking on these guarantees. They had priced these guarantees at their cost, and now it seemed likely that their costs were going to be much higher than they had projected. This meant the annuities they had written might actually lose the insurance companies money.

The insurance companies *couldn't take away* the contracts they had already agreed to (the ones that many of our clients bought), but they *could* decide to stop selling these kinds of benefits going forward. And that is what several insurance companies decided to do.

Many insurance companies decided that they were done selling contracts with living benefits. However, many others decided that they could still offer these living benefits, but they had to charge more and/or promise less.

Some hedged their risk in the new contracts by limiting investors to more conservative investment choices. Others simply raised the fee for the living benefit[18] to equal what they anticipated

---

[18] Reminder: *Living benefit* is the term used to describe the new add-on insurance that guarantees the investor a minimum income or withdrawal benefit during their lifetime without giving up the remainder of their money upon death. These were often added to annuity contracts through the use of a *rider*, an insurance term that describes an optional insurance benefit that is added to a regular insurance contract.

the new actual costs to be. Others reduced the withdrawal percentage that they were going to guarantee for a lifetime. There were many other contractual changes as well.

Through all of this, the financial advisor (who was acting as a fiduciary) *had to become an insurance contract expert.* We had to keep up on all the changes and constantly analyze the best contracts for our clients as we made recommendations. Moreover, we *had* to tell them about these guaranteed options; if we didn't tell them, then we weren't fulfilling our fiduciary duty. After all, if it was in our client's best interest to have the highest guaranteed lifetime income stream that they could receive, then the annuity was the only option that could provide that.

The media and the regulators weren't really keeping up with these rapid changes. Remembering the history of annuities from the '70s and '80s, they saw all this annuity activity and cried foul. Therefore, the tides were heavily against the financial advisor fiduciary. They had two choices: (1) learn to be an insurance contract expert and fight the negative image of annuities as they educated their clients on their options while letting the clients choose a guaranteed strategy versus a non-guaranteed strategy or (2) join the crowd of media "gurus" and regulators and decry these annuities as bad so they could avoid the time investment and mental energy of becoming an insurance contract expert. (By the way, this freed them up to make a lot of money by selling the popular thing to buy: managed money accounts.)

We do not believe that annuities are better than managed money (or vice versa for that matter). Please hear me when I say this. It is hard to read all the above information and believe that we are truly unbiased about annuities, but we simply believe that our clients deserve to know *all their options* when they decide to invest their life savings. Just because it is more popular and easier to ignore annuities doesn't mean that it is the right thing to do.

We fought the fight, and we educated our clients. After they understood how annuities worked, many of our clients chose to use annuities as a significant part of their retirement portfolio. This, of course, made the 2008 financial crisis much easier to get through emotionally for our clients. And it provided them with the peace of mind to know that their income from their annuities would never go away. They were guaranteed to not run out of money.

Unfortunately, however, not every investor received a clear description of annuities this past two decades. Over the past hundred years, annuities have gotten *a lot* more complicated, and with that complication there is always an opportunity for misunderstandings, mistakes, and disappointment. Unfortunately, the history of annuities doesn't end with simple errors. There are a handful of unscrupulous individuals who used the complicated nature of annuities to sell this type of insurance to many investors who didn't understand what they were buying. When it came to annuities, the actions of the few bad apples had the impact of poisoning the barrel of public opinion.

Like most news and media coverage, stories that frighten us will always grab the attention of our self-preservation instincts. This gives the story-pushers more of our focus and increases their ratings. In this way, it is actually our own fault that we are assaulted by so much negativity in the news. As many of my clients have heard me say, "With two TVs in a crowded room airing two different scenes, the crowd will always watch a plane crash over a puppy frolicking in a field of flowers."

Hence, the handful of stories about advisors abusing their position of trust and taking advantage of the poor, unsuspecting public have frightened many investors against annuities. They have scared so many of these people about annuities that even several well-known financial gurus won't touch them with a ten-foot pole.

And why should they? For a financial advisor, talking about annuities is an uphill and mostly losing battle. It has been much easier to go with the flow and argue against annuities. The regulators wanted us to stop selling them.[19] There are countless financial advisors preying on the anti-annuity movement to frighten clients into their offices as a way to make the client hire them to manage their assets. After all, it is almost impossible to get through the non-guaranteed strategies without the use of an experienced and qualified financial advisor. Avoiding annuities is a surefire way to make sure that you (the client) are dependent on them (the anti-annuity advisor) as your financial advisor for the rest of your life.

And annuities are complicated. If you can't explain them well to a client, then there is a lot of opportunity for a client to get confused. Confusion leads to disappointment, negative

---

[19] They were exhausted from the anti-annuity 403b backlash they had to deal with in the late 1980s and early 1990s, and they weren't as up to speed on the new living benefits. There is always a delay in understanding new investments and insurance modifications, and regulators are usually on the tail end of that learning curve. Most regulators are just now starting to become pro-annuity as they are learning more about the advantages of these living benefits.

surprises, and lawsuits. Also, annuities often used to pay the selling advisor a commission of 4 percent to 6 percent one time on the sale.[20] That means that these advisors only got paid once. If a person recommended a managed money investment portfolio to you, then they could earn 1 percent of the assets under management for the next several decades. So what incentive did they have to teach you about annuities? Why would they risk twenty to thirty years of income, their career, and public ridicule to do that?

The answer: Because it's the right thing to do.

I have witnessed the firsthand emotional benefits of clients not needing to worry about running out of money. When that fear is erased from their minds, they are able to *really* enjoy retirement.

Our mission at Clear Financial Partners is *"We empower our clients and associates in their journey to achieve their unique vision of Happiness."*

---

[20] Fortunately, most insurance companies have added a commission choice to their products that now allows a financial advisor to choose a much lower up-front compensation and instead choose a trailing revenue structure that is similar to the 1 percent per year that most managed-money-oriented financial advisors charge. This has leveled the playing field for recommendations and greatly lessened the conflict of interest for those recommending annuities versus managed money. If you work with an advisor who helps you purchase an annuity, be sure that your representative is choosing the 1 percent (or similar) trailing commission option (as we do) when they set up your account. This will ensure that they will receive ongoing compensation to service you in an amount similar to what they would receive if you chose a managed-money investment portfolio. This choice doesn't cost you any extra, but an advisor who chooses the high up-front commission with little to no ongoing compensation will have little to no financial incentive to keep serving you for the lifetime of your contract.

How can we ignore teaching about annuities? We can all see firsthand how much peace of mind they can bring our clients.

Fortunately, the answer to that question is "We can't."

This is why the sale of annuities has risen drastically over the last two decades. This is why the evolution of annuities has transformed these products into the diverse creation that they are today. There is an insatiable demand from retirees over the past two decades for an investment that guarantees them they cannot run out of money in retirement while still providing them upside potential for growth, a minimum income they can count on, and (in many cases) the opportunity to leave behind any unused assets to their heirs. It is because of this demand by the public combined with the loyalty of the fiduciary advisor that has led to the abundant environment of annuity products that we have today.

But, it is a complicated universe to navigate. And, like the bucket strategy or the other myriad of investment approaches for your 401k, choosing the right annuity strategy is best done with the advice and assistance from an advisor who is extremely well educated and experienced with annuities.

CHAPTER

SO HOW MUCH DO I PUT
INTO AN ANNUITY?

We have explored the history of annuities, and we have touched on the basics of what they do. But what now? How much money do we put in an annuity? What kind of annuity do we use? What kind of annuities are there?

The answer to "How much do I put into an annuity?" is—like many of the other answers—"*It depends*."

What type of annuity should you put your money into?—It depends.

While annuities can provide a high amount of guaranteed lifetime income, they are also much less liquid. They have penalties if you take more than the allowed amounts. Some of these annuities have significant annual fees and surrender charges, while others will restrict your growth to a more conservative amount of earnings potential than a traditional investment portfolio.

If we make some assumptions, then we can get closer to an answer to this chapter's question.

If these costs, the lack of liquidity, or any other reasons make you conclude that annuities aren't right for you, then your answer is *none*. Don't put anything into an annuity if you aren't comfortable with this type of investment.

However, if you want *some* amount of guaranteed income that you cannot outlive, then you will have to put *something* into annuities. So how much? Maybe you can solve this problem by solving for the gap between your current guaranteed lifetime income and how much guaranteed lifetime income you want.

Let's assume that you have found an annuity strategy that will produce a 5 percent annual distribution from your contract that is guaranteed for as long as you live. Let's further assume that it will provide the same income for your spouse as long as he/she lives after you die. Then let's assume that if you and your spouse die and have any money left in the annuity, the leftovers will go to your heirs.

This type of annuity strategy exists, and it can be found in either variable annuities or fixed indexed annuities with some good shopping (and the help of a good advisor).[21]

---

[21] At Clear Financial Partners, we are (of course) accepting new clients all the time. If you would like our help, you can reach us at 503-579-1000, on our website at www.clearfp.com, via email at info@clearfp.com, or in our app *ClearFP: The Clock*. If you are already working with a phenomenal advisor, then please stay with them. We want you to have the right person for you. But if you need someone or don't have the right someone, we are happy to help.

If we make the above assumptions, then the answer to this chapter's question is: as much as you are comfortable tying up in an investment with these qualities.

If you have Social Security benefits and pensions that total $40,000 per year, and you want to live on $100,000 per year, then you have a $60,000 gap in your desired income. You might want to invest $1.2 million into an annuity strategy like the one mentioned above. After all, $1.2 million invested with a 5 percent annual distribution would fill in the gap of $60,000 per year. When added to your Social Security income, you now have $100,000 of guaranteed lifetime income.[22]

If you have $2 million in your 401k, then you might put the $1.2 million in the annuity strategy and put the other $800,000 into different investment strategies for other purposes.

What if you only have $800,000? Now the same investment is only going to produce $40,000 per year of annual income on top of the $40,000 from Social Security. This brings your income to $80,000 total, but you wanted $100,000. What should you do?

Face the facts. You probably need to work longer, save more money, plan to live a short life, or expect to drain your account to zero before you die. If you don't like the above options, then you need to get used to living on a lower amount of money. Learn to live on $80,000 instead of $100,000 per year.

---

[22] Don't forget to anticipate inflation down the road. Some annuity benefits will increase once you have turned them on, but most annuity payments are not designed to go up once they begin. Be sure to fully understand the most likely income to reasonably expect from your annuity *in addition* to the extreme best case and worst scenarios of how your annuity could perform as well.

The reasonable withdrawal percentage that we discussed in chapter 3 never gets above 5 percent per year. More than that is an unreasonable withdrawal percentage for any traditional investment strategies (guaranteed or non-guaranteed).

If you would like to get a sense of where you stand financially, you should try downloading our free application for your phone or tablet. Just search "ClearFP" in your app store, and you can learn more about building your own financial plan. You can build a plan for yourself that is identical to the plans we use with our clients every day. We call the image of your plan your *ClearFP Clock*.

CHAPTER

SO...NOW...WHAT DO I
DO WITH MY 401K?

Here are the short answers:

1. If you are more than ten years away from retirement, then you should maximize your 401k contributions. Keep it invested in a diversified portfolio that is as aggressive as you feel is right for your risk tolerance. (All 401k plans have risk profile questionnaires that will help you figure out your personal risk tolerance.)
2. If you have an old 401k from a previous employer, then you should consider rolling it over to an IRA (individual retirement account). There are pros and cons that are best discussed with a financial advisor, but most people roll over their 401k's to IRA accounts after they leave their prior employers. The investment options in your 401k are limited to the selections that your former employer has chosen for its company; however, you can choose any investments you want (including annuities) inside your own IRA. It is important to be aware of a few additional differences between IRAs

and your 401k. ([1] The 401k may have lower costs due to negotiated rates that your employer has garnered. [2] The 401k has the unique ability to be accessed without the 10 percent penalty if you retire after age fifty-five, whereas the IRA will require you to wait until fifty-nine and a half or to use a 72T distribution strategy.[23] [3] If you have a Roth IRA conversion strategy or backdoor Roth strategy, there may be advantages to having less money in IRAs when doing your converting.) Other than those issues and a few other subtleties, the advantages of consolidating your 401k's into one IRA that you control usually outweigh the disadvantages. The primary advantage is that it is generally simpler to monitor and manage. Also, the flexibility of investment options are usually more desirable than leaving the money in your 401k plans after you have terminated your employment.

3. If you are less than ten years away from reaching financial independence or are over the age of fifty-five, then you should seriously consider moving out of the *accumulation phase* and start getting ready for the *preservation phase* of your asset management cycle. You don't have the time to handle major volatility. It's time to consider getting more conservative with the money you have accumulated and start deciding whether you are going to use an annuity

---

[23] A 72T distribution strategy is a special provision in the tax code that allows withdrawals from IRA's before the age of fifty-nine and a half years old *without incurring the ten percent penalty tax.* There are very specific rules and restrictions with severe consequences if they are not followed. If you choose to use this strategy, you should be sure to consult your tax advisor and financial advisor regularly to assure that you are complying with the regulations.

strategy. If you haven't had a financial planner thus far, start thinking about building a relationship with one. The accumulation phase is much simpler than the *preservation phase* and the imminent *distribution phase* that is coming.

Remember—even though you are getting more conservative and prepared with the money you have accumulated, it is important to continue with aggressive saving in these final catch-up years before you retire. There is less time to maneuver your plan, so these are the final adjustments you can make that will cement your retirement income plan for the rest of your life. Pay attention. Have a plan. Take control of your situation.

4. If you are fifty-nine and a half or older, you should be looking at taking an *in-service distribution* to roll over your 401k while you are still working. Your money has been tied up at your employer's retirement account for all your working years, but you can now move it into an IRA and take control. There are no more excuses. Whether you do this alone or seek assistance from a financial advisor, you need to start making decisions. Take a look at how much money you have saved so far. What is your income plan? How much Social Security income will you have? Do you have other income sources? Pensions? Rental or business income? Royalties? How much do you want to keep liquid for emergencies? How much fun money do you want to just blow on special things? Have you considered the extra medical costs coming your way? If you are planning to retire before sixty-five, what is your pre-Medicare plan for health insurance? Do you know how much that will cost? If you do have a pension, which

survivorship option are you going to choose? When do you take Social Security? How is your health? How is your spouse's health? How many years will you live? How much money do you want to leave behind as a legacy? Do you have heirs to leave it to? A charity? What happens to your life insurance after you retire? Do you still need some? Is your house paid off? Will you stay in the same home? Do you want a vacation home? Who will take care of you if you need long-term care? Who is helping to take care of your parents? What about your grandkids' college expenses? Can you help? Should you help? How should you help? What if you live past one hundred and are actually healthy and happy? Do you have a plan for that?

It is easy to see why many people simply freak out, keep working, and postpone answering these questions. It can be daunting to think about even one of these answers.

Retirement readiness isn't just having enough money to retire. Retirement readiness is also about being mentally prepared to deal with these questions and having plans in place that answer these questions in a way that makes you happy.

Most financial advisors earn about 1 percent of the assets under management per year. If you invest $1 million with them, then they will earn about $10,000 per year to help you with that $1 million. Out of that $10,000 they pay for their staff; they pay for their insurance; and they pay for their licenses, software, and all their other business expenses to provide you with a personal chief financial officer to guide you through all these answers. Many investments can move up or down by more than 1 percent in a single day.

I always say that if I didn't earn my clients at least an extra 1 percent or save them an extra 1 percent on the money they have invested with me, then how could I justify my occupation? How could I sleep at night?

A good financial advisor should always be more valuable than they cost. According to a research study undertaken by the Vanguard Group, a good financial advisor adds about 3 percent to your annual return.[24] (At the time the company undertook this study, they didn't even offer financial advisors as part of their business model.) With this kind of evidence, why wouldn't everyone seek out a financial advisor?

Of course, this doesn't mean that an advisor will always make you money. And, it doesn't mean that you should earn a higher return than the markets. It just means that advice from a professional should help you do much better in your planning than you would have done without them. Sometimes, they may earn you *less* money than you would have earned without them, but they may have helped you take *much less risk* than you would have otherwise taken.

Find a professional who you can have a good relationship with. Commit to working with someone for a year. Then, look back at the end of the year and decide whether you felt the relationship was worthwhile. If it was, keep working with them. If not, then find someone else.

There are a lot of amazing people out there who are educated to help you answer the questions above. Let them help you conquer your challenges with retirement readiness.

---

[24] "Putting a Value on Value: Quantifying Advisor's Alpha," Published August 31, 2016.

CONCLUSION

There are an infinite number of money-related questions that could be asked. Moreover, there are an infinite number of possible scenarios that every client can encounter. The only guarantee is that *your situation is different than anyone and everyone else's situation.*

One of the most common misconceptions about financial advisors is that you need to have a lot of money to work with one. This just isn't true.

Many advisors, including us at Clear Financial Partners, have low account minimums (our firm's is currently $250,000). Many advisors have adjusted service models so that they can still provide help at a reasonable price for most people who are serious about improving their financial situation.

Most advisors who manage wealth for their clients earn about 1 percent of the assets under management per year. This aligns them with your best interests. *They earn more money when you earn more money; and, they earn less money when you earn less money.* Even advisors who work with annuity accounts often choose a commission option which pays them very little up front and 1 percent of the assets under management per year. By choosing this commission option, the advisor is making sure that they are incentivized to serve you for as long as you choose to keep working with them. And if you don't like who you are working with, you can usually change agents and just shift that 1 percent earnings to a new advisor. This means that *your advisor has to keep earning your business every year.*

Over the past twenty-five years, I have been extremely fortunate to build deep relationships with many of the clients I serve. Most human beings would count themselves lucky if they were able to have just one of these types of relationships in their lifetime. I have had dozens. *My clients are my family.*

If you don't have someone in your life like this—if you don't have an advisor who you trust like a son or daughter; a mother or father; a husband or wife; or the most loved, revered, and trusted family member you have ever known—then I would challenge you to find them. They are out there. I've met thousands of amazing financial advisors from countries all over the world through my career. I have had the wonderful opportunity to get to know many of these advisors just as deeply as some of my clients over the past twenty-two years. They are some of the most selfless individuals that I have ever met.

And if you still aren't ready to reach out to an advisor and have this type of a relationship, you can at least download and work with our free app: *ClearFP: The Clock.* We launched it in the middle of 2018, and we will keep making improvements to help you.

Keep learning. Keep an eye on your money. The only two limited resources we all have are our minutes and our dollars.

Take good care of your dollars so that you can get the best return on your minutes that this life can bring you.

Sincerely,

Tim Clairmont

COMMON INVESTMENT
QUESTIONS WITH
EASY-TO-UNDERSTAND ANSWERS

Common Investment Questions with Easy-to-Understand Answers

Like so many things in life, the investing world can appear complicated. But once something is understood, it can't be unlearned.

Below are easy-to-understand answers to questions that are commonly wondered and occasionally asked.

You don't have to be embarrassed for asking. You don't have to worry about what someone thinks of you. You don't have to tell anyone that you don't know what an ETF is or what the S&P 500 is.

Just read the answers below, and you will know more than the vast majority of the public (even if they pretend to understand these things at a dinner party).

What is "buy and hold" all about, and why don't advisors recommend selling before the market goes down? (Strategic Investing vs. Tactical Investing)

You've heard the term *buy and hold*, but what is this strategy really about? Why don't financial advisors simply get you out of the market before it goes down and then back in again when it's about to go up?

The answer is pretty simple. There are two types of investors in the world: people who think you *can* time the market and people who think you *can't* time the market.

Lots of very smart people spent hours of their lives and lots of money trying to determine the answer to this question: Can you time the market?

Strategic Investing—for those who believe you *can't* time the market

The primary assumption that a buy and hold strategy depends on is that the stock market is pretty efficient at accurately pricing stocks all the time.

In other words, at any given moment, the price of a stock is *fair*. It accurately represents all the hopes and fears of the general public about that particular company. It accurately reflects reasonable expectations for the future value of currency in the country or countries where that company does business. It accurately reflects current expectations about interest rates, political climate, cost of goods and services, and all other things that might impact the value of that particular security at that moment in time.

If you believe that these stock prices are *always* fair and accurate, then there is no way to accurately predict with any amount of certainty the future changes in the price of any stock. If you believe that this is true, then there is no way to buy something at a *deal*, and there is also no way to *overpay* for stock in a company. You will always get a *fair* price. Therefore, the only way to make money with this belief set is to buy the security at a fair price now, hold it over time, and sell it for a fair price down the road. You just hope the price down the road is higher than what you paid for it.

If you are worried about the particular performance of one company, then you would make sure to own multiple companies in your portfolio. This way, if one company goes down in value, then you hope another company will go up to offset it.

Ultimately, a theory arose that described this reasonable way to invest for those people who came to believe that you just cannot time the market with any degree of consistent success. That theory is known as modern portfolio theory. As a *theory*, it is just an idea or an opinion; it is not a *law* or a *rule*. Like all theories, the idea is based on some assumptions. But what is the bottom line?

The bottom line is this: if you think any one company might not do well but the overall performance of all companies together will likely rise over time, then you can own a little piece of all the companies and rise with the economy as a whole. This is the basic foundation of the idea behind diversification.

Moreover, if you think that investors must be rewarded more for taking more risk (otherwise they wouldn't take more risk than they needed to), then you should expect higher long-term average returns from riskier assets. You have to expect to get a greater return in exchange for your willingness to take greater risk.

Again, this type of investing is referred to as buy and hold or strategic investing. Its core belief is that your success in investing is about time *in* the market, not *timing* the market.

Tactical Investing—for those who believe you can time the market

On the other hand, if you believe that markets are inefficient (that there are errors in the pricing that with research and insight you can exploit), then you will purchase stocks when they are priced incorrectly at a discount and you will sell them later for a profit when they are worth more money. Or, if you believe that you can accurately predict the future value of a company better than most of the rest of the world, then you would believe that you could take advantage of that knowledge by buying stocks when they are worth less and selling them when they are worth more.

This type of investing is known as timing the market or tactical investing.

There are varying degrees of tactical investing. Some managers will try to completely predict the up and down movements of the markets. They will go to cash (a zero-return but zero-loss position) when they think the market will go down, and then they will try to buy things at the low and enjoy the rise as the market goes back up. Some investors will even make bets on the market going down by *shorting* a stock. These are *extreme* examples of market timing and/or tactical investing.

There are milder examples of tactical investing where portfolio managers will get out of a particular asset class when they believe it will do poorly in the near future. For example, if you knew that oil prices were going to plummet, then you might want to sell all your stock in companies that profit from the price of oil being higher. Or if you believed that the United States stock market was going to go down, you might move your whole portfolio overseas. This type of market timing/tactical investment stems from predicting the future performance of a whole group of companies as opposed to any one particular company. There is very little evidence to support that this type of market timing/tactical investing is likely to be consistently repeatable either. It seems that predicting the future performance of a group of securities or particular asset class is just about as challenging as predicting the future performance of any one stock.

In the mildest forms of market timing/tactical investing, you will see portfolio managers make slight adjustments to try to avoid generally unfavorable securities or markets and to increase their exposure to securities and/or markets that they believe will do well. There is some evidence that this type of behavior can potentially add value by decreasing risk and/or improving return for many portfolios. But it still isn't easily replicable.

All investors need to decide what they believe in and which type of investing approach they want to use with their own money. It is in your best interest to make sure that your philosophy about investing is aligned with the philosophy of your chosen financial advisor. If you believe in buy and hold whereas your financial advisor believes in market timing, then you are likely to become frustrated with the advice you receive. Likewise, the opposite is true; if you believe that your advisor should be able to predict the future and time the market, then you might become frustrated when your advisor advises you to just *ride through* or *hold* when you believe you should be buying or selling. Even if you and your financial advisor disagree on strategic versus tactical investing, you should at least make sure that the money manager you choose (which may be different from your financial advisor) is investing with the same philosophy that you believe in. It is *your* money after all.

What is a leading economic indicator, and why can't we easily predict when the market is going to go down?

Economic indicators are statistics that economists use to try to determine how good or bad an economy is doing. Some indicators are *leading* indicators—meaning that these indicate where the economy's future may be heading. Other indicators are *lagging* indicators—meaning these indicators show where the economy has just been.

In general, most economists believe the stock market is a leading economic indicator. This is why it is so hard to predict. After all, if the stock market shows us where our economy is heading, then looking at an economy's current statistics is likely to only reflect what the stock market has just done. You might as well be reading tea leaves to predict the stock market!

On the other hand, unemployment is generally believed to be a lagging economic indicator. This means that we can look at the unemployment rate to get a sense of where our economy has just been. Alternatively, we can look at our current economy to see where unemployment is likely to go.

What are the S&P 500, the Dow, and the Nasdaq?

When you want to get an idea about how a large market is performing, the best way to check on that is by looking at an *index*.[25] An index is just a group of investments that are very clearly defined so that no one can arbitrarily change them. If you ever did a science lab experiment in high school, you may remember that there was always a control group. This is the group that is kept in a constant state so that you can compare your experiment with the control. Indexes are like the control group for checking to see how your personal investment portfolio (your experiment) is doing.

Imagine that you just wanted to know how the biggest thirty companies in the United States have been doing. How have their stocks performed over time? Maybe you own shares (stock) in one of those companies, and you are wondering if you have performed similarly or differently from the other big twenty-nine companies in the United States. This is the basic definition of the Dow[26]. The Dow Jones Industrial Average is just an average of the value of the biggest thirty companies in the United States.

---

[25] Indexes are unmanaged, and investors cannot invest directly in an index.

[26] The Dow Jones Industrial Average (DJIA) is a price-weighted average of thirty actively traded blue chip stocks, primarily industrials but including financials and other service-oriented companies. The components, which change from time to time, represent between 15 and 20 percent of the market value of NYSE stocks.

What if you wanted to know how the biggest five hundred companies in the United States were doing? You guessed it—that's what the S&P 500[27] is.

So what is the Nasdaq? The Nasdaq is an acronym that stands for the National Association of Securities Dealer's Automated Quotation System. This is actually a stock exchange (a place where buyers and sellers can trade ownership of stocks). The other two (larger) stock exchanges—NYSE (New York Stock Exchange) and NYSE American (formerly known as the American Stock Exchange - AMEX)—have rules about minimum company sizes before a company's stock can officially be bought and sold in these exchanges. They are only for the big companies (Coca-Cola, Disney, and the like). The Nasdaq[28] is an automated online stock exchange that allows smaller publicly traded companies (the ones that don't meet the minimum-size requirements of the other two exchanges) to still find a place for buyers and sellers to trade shares. Therefore, when people refer to the value of the Nasdaq, they are using it as an index that measures the total average value of all the *smaller* companies that trade within the Unites States. Many look at this as the control

---

[27] The Standard & Poor's 500 (S&P 500) is an unmanaged group of securities considered to be representative of the stock market in general. It is a market-value weighted index with each stock's weight in the index proportionate to its market value.

[28] The Nasdaq Composite Index is a market-capitalization weighted index of the more than three thousand common equities listed on the Nasdaq stock exchange. The types of securities in the index include American depository receipts, common stocks, real estate investment trusts (REITs), and tracking stocks. The index includes all Nasdaq listed stocks that are not derivatives, preferred shares, funds, exchange-traded funds (ETFs), or debentures.

group to measure the performance of investments in smaller companies within the Unites States.

What about international investing? There are indexes for those too. The EAFE[29] is an index that measures the approximate value of all the stock trading on the major exchanges in Europe, Australasia, and the Far East. What about China and other *emerging markets*? They have their own indexes as well. For example: The Hang Seng[30]index is commonly looked at to see how Hong Kong is doing.

All of these indexes are just the control groups that investors can look at to see how a larger segment of the investing world is performing.

This is also why it is unfair to measure the performance of your international portfolio (experiment) against the domestic indexes (control group) like the S&P 500. They are totally different markets. You should expect them to perform differently.

One comment about the S&P 500 index: the S&P 500 is a *weighted index*. So what is a weighted index?

---

[29] The MSCI EAFE Index (Europe, Australasia, Far East) is a free-float-adjusted market capitalization index that is designed to measure the equity market performance of developed markets, excluding the United States and Canada.

[30] The Hang Seng Index is a free-float-adjusted market-capitalization-weighted stock market index in Hong Kong. It is used to record and monitor daily changes of the largest companies of the Hong Kong stock market and is the main indicator of the overall market performance in Hong Kong. These fifty constituent companies represent about 58 percent of the capitalization of the Hong Kong Stock Exchange.

Imagine that you had a giant jar containing five hundred marbles. Each marble represents one of the biggest five hundred companies in the United States. Got the picture?

You might think that all the marbles in your jar are the same size. Most people would envision similarly sized marbles. But the S&P 500 has marbles that are proportionate to the *size* of the company. For example, X is currently one of the ten largest companies in the Unites States. Y is currently ranked near the 450th largest company in the Unites States.

When the gurus at Standard and Poor's decided to build the S&P 500 index, they believed that it would more accurately reflect the growth of the US economy if they gave more weight to the bigger companies and less weight to the smaller ones. If we stay with the analogy of the jar of marbles, then this means that the marble representing X could be as much as one hundred times larger than the one for Y. To put it another way, if Y was a standard-sized marble, then X would be a marble that is approximately the size of a baseball!

What are index funds, ETFs, and actively managed funds?

We talked about what a mutual fund was in chapter 4, but what is the difference between index funds, ETFs (exchange traded funds), and actively managed funds?[31]

Let's start with index funds. First of all, there is no way to invest directly into an index. That's right—when you put your money into an S&P 500 index fund, you are not investing your money directly into the S&P 500 index.

The S&P 500 index is just a control group that we use to measure the historical performance of a particular group of companies. An S&P 500 index *fund* is a mutual fund that is *trying* to match the performance of the S&P 500 index.

The S&P 500 has very clear, very strict rules that define how to calculate the value of the index at any given moment. However, the real life process of buying stocks in the 500 biggest companies in the United States in a proportionate weighting to the size of each company relative to the size of the other 499 largest companies in the United States is a little harder to implement.

Just think about it. There is the cost of buying and selling the stocks themselves; the index doesn't reflect that. Then the relative size of each company when compared to the other 499 is constantly changing; how do you adjust the stocks that

[31] Mutual funds and exchange traded funds (ETFs) are sold by prospectus. Please consider the investment objectives, risks, charges, and expenses carefully before investing. The prospectus, which contains this and other information about the investment company, can be obtained from the fund company or your financial professional. Be sure to read the prospectus carefully before deciding whether to invest.

the fund owns at any given moment to more closely resemble the S&P 500 index? What happens when a bunch of money comes into the S&P 500 fund? All that money needs to buy into the stocks on that day. Which ones do they buy? How has the index changed from the previous day? Has it changed? What if a large group of investors want to take their money out at the same time? Which stocks have to get sold? How much of each stock?

Fortunately, computers and automated buying and selling programs allow most of the S&P 500 index funds to match the S&P 500 index pretty closely. But they are still *funds*. Other indexes are harder to mimic more exactly in real life. Generally, the more money that is invested in a particular market, the easier it is to mimic the index for that market.

So what is the difference between an actively managed fund and an index fund? The easiest way to explain that is with another analogy.

Imagine an apple orchard. There are five hundred trees in this apple orchard. Got it? Picture it clearly. Now, each one of these trees represents one of the biggest five hundred companies in the United States. (Kind of like the jar of marbles from above, right?)

Now, in the next part of the story, you have an apple picker. This person has a barrel and is going to walk through the orchard and take one apple from every tree and put it in the barrel. This barrel represents the S&P 500 index fund mentioned above. (Forget about the weighted index stuff from above and ignore the differences in the size of the apples relative to each other for now.)

In the next part of the story we bring in a second apple picker. This picker is going to go through your orchard and also put five hundred apples in the barrel. But the second picker is going to take a different number of apples from certain trees. The second picker might like the apples on one tree better than another, so three apples are picked from that tree for the barrel. The next tree doesn't look as good to the second apple picker, so that tree is skipped.

At the end of the day, you have two barrels of five hundred apples from the same orchard. What's the difference? One has a single apple from every tree, and the other has the apples chosen by the second apple picker. The first barrel is an *index fund*, and the second barrel is an *actively managed fund*. See the difference?

By the way, which apple barrel do you think was probably cheaper to produce? That's right—the index fund was cheaper. Why? Because you had to pay the second apple picker to think. The second apple picker had to use his or her brain or some other special approach to investing to try to decide which apples to take from which trees. The first apple picker was able to simply follow the easy rules of the S&P 500—*no thinking!* Actively managed funds have higher internal expenses than most index funds that invest in the same orchard. This is why actively managed funds generally cost the investor more than index funds (they have higher internal expense ratios).

Of course, this higher cost also means that the second apple picker needs to outperform the first apple picker *by at least as much as the higher cost* in order to justify an investor's decision to pay the second apple picker to think. The second apple picker needs to outperform the extra cost, otherwise, why would any investor use their fund?

So how do international funds compare with the S&P 500 in this analogy? They are like a totally different orchard of fruit. Think of international investing (like the EAFE) as if it were an orange grove. The emerging market index might be a cherry orchard. Ultimately, statistics have shown that the mix of the types of fruit in the basket (the asset allocation)[32] has been much more responsible for long-term investment performance than the specific selection of apples from certain trees. But past performance doesn't necessarily indicate future results. It is up to you to decide how to use this information for your investing. (On a side point, isn't this a little exciting? If we could predict things like the stock market and the weather, then what surprises would be left to us in life anyway?)

Oh yeah ... ETFs. So an ETF is actually a modification of an index fund that allows investors to trade their mutual fund shares more frequently. I know that can be confusing; stay with me for a moment.

Mutual funds (open end mutual funds, anyway) are required to *settle up* every day. After all, with a portfolio manager actively buying and selling different stocks and bonds on a particular day, how can investors really *know* how much their portions of the mutual fund are worth?

The rules of investing in mutual funds say that every (open end) mutual fund that is available to the general public must

---

[32] Neither asset allocation nor diversification guarantee a profit or protect against a loss in a declining market. They are methods used to help manage investment risk.

publish its price per share (its NAV or net asset value) at the end of each day that the stock market is open. This means that investors who want to buy or sell a share of a particular mutual fund can *only buy or sell at the end of each market close.*

So what happens if the stock market is moving a lot in the middle of the day, and an investor wants to get in or get out before the market closes?

With mutual funds, the answer to the above question is *tough luck.* You have to wait till the end of the day. But with the evolution of computers and the easier, more automated way that certain portfolios of index funds are run, the value of many index funds can be very rapidly calculated in the middle of the trading day.

So what is an ETF (exchange traded fund)? It is basically a mutual fund that can be traded like a stock on one of the stock exchanges. This means that investors can get in or get out any time that the stock market is open. This ease of buying and selling shares of ETFs has generally made ETFs very popular with investors and portfolio managers who are trying to use a very liquid investment with relatively lower internal expenses that tries to mimic a particular market index.

What are asset allocation funds, balanced funds, age-weighted funds, and target-date retirement funds?

How do you decide on your asset allocation? Or to stay with the analogy above, how do you choose your fruit basket?

Many economists and statisticians have estimated that your asset allocation mix (the composition of your fruit basket) is responsible for over 90 percent of your investment performance! So how do you build your basket? Do you fill it with half apples, a quarter oranges, and a quarter cherries? What about the pears and the kiwis?

Fortunately, some investment companies have tried to make this choice easier for you.

They've already built these one-stop-shop types of mutual funds listed above.

An asset allocation fund is just a fund that tries to mix together different kinds of fruit for you in an overall blend that the fund manager likes. Typically, this type of basket will have some US stocks (some bigger ones and some smaller ones), some international stocks (often from both developed countries and emerging markets), and some bonds (both government and corporate bonds). By diversifying your portfolio in one fund, this type of fund can give you access to a wider variety of fruit in your fruit basket, and this variety is typically achieved with a much lower investment minimum. Perhaps you just want someone else to decide your fruit basket mix for you? Then this type of fund takes a crack at it.

Balanced funds are a more specific type of asset allocation fund that tries to blend all of the different categories in a more middle-of-the-road kind of way. They are usually balancing pretty similar amounts of stock and bonds.

Age-weighted funds are another type of asset allocation fund. This one is designed with the premise that as you get older you will likely get more conservative. Therefore, if you choose a fund with a younger age weighting, then you will likely have a higher percentage in stocks than bonds. Then as time goes by (and you get older), the portfolio manager will automatically adjust your overall asset allocation (fruit basket mix) to include fewer stocks and more bonds.

Target-date funds are another type of dynamic/changing asset allocation fund. This type of fund tries to change its mix based on how far away the investor is from using the money. For example, consider an investor who is saving in a 401k. The investor is currently thirty years old, and has a target date for retirement at sixty years old. What will the date be when the investor is sixty years old? Right now, that would be about 2053. So the investor might choose a target date fund labeled the 2050, 2055, or 2060 Fund. This would likely have more stocks than bonds. A 2020 or 2025 target-date fund would imply that the investor was going to use the money very soon; consequently, the portfolio manager would likely have very few stocks and likely a large amount of cash and/or short-term bonds.

At the end of the day, your decision on your asset allocation is very important. This is one of the primary advantages that you can gain in working with a financial advisor and/or a professional money manager. Most advisors and economists believe that a good asset allocation can gain the same rate of return as many other portfolios while taking less risk. Or, vice versa, they believe that a good asset allocation can get a higher rate of return while taking the same risk as other lower performing portfolios. This is the fundamental precept behind modern portfolio theory's concept of the efficient frontier.

How do we know if an actively managed fund is any good?
(What are alpha, beta, expected return, and R-squared?)

When financial advisors and investors are trying to determine whether or not a mutual fund is a "good" fund or a "bad" fund, they look at certain statistics. You might imagine that a good place to start is to find an index to compare your fund to. In general, that is usually where most of these types of analyses begin. If you decide that you want to analyze your funds or your overall investment portfolio to try to determine if it is good or bad, then you will need to follow a process similar to the one that follows.

Step 1: First, you try to find the index that most closely resembles the investment that you are analyzing. If you are investing in a large-cap domestic fund (stock in large companies in the United States) or a midcap domestic fund (stock in medium-size companies in the United States), then you might consider comparing these funds to the S&P 500.

What if you chose the wrong index? What would happen if you compared your US large-cap fund to the EAFE index (Europe, Australia, and the Far East), for example?

Our common sense tells us that this wouldn't be a fair comparison, but is there a statistic that would have shown us that this isn't fair? Yes, there is. That statistic is "R^2" (R-squared).

This statistic is referred to as the *correlation coefficient*. This measures how close the relationship is between two portfolios that are being compared. In our case, we are comparing your investment fund (the experiment) to the index (the control). If the correlation coefficient (R^2) was a 1.0, then that would mean that the two funds being compared are perfectly correlated: When one goes up, the other goes up 100 percent of the time. And when one goes down, the other goes down 100 percent of the time.

In the real world, it is very challenging to get two funds that are perfectly correlated. Generally speaking, a correlation coefficient above a 90 or 95 (an R^2 equal to 0.90 or 0.95) would be considered extremely well correlated. This means that the two portfolios move in the same direction 90 percent or 95 percent of the time. Anything below a 70 (an R^2 equal to 0.70 or less) would be considered not very well correlated. If they only move in the same direction 70 percent of the time or less, then it is very hard to anticipate anything that might happen in your investment (experiment) by looking at this particular portfolio (control). In other words, if you are comparing your investment to an index with a correlation coefficient below 70, then you are pretty much wasting your time. It would be unreasonable to expect one fund to go up or down when the other is going up or down because there is no obvious statistical correlation. Furthermore, all the other statistics that follow (alpha, beta, and expected return) would be unreliable for any aspect of statistical analysis.

When you are comparing a fund/investment to an index and find a comparison with a higher correlation coefficient than any other index, then you are said to have found the *most closely fit index*. Finding the most closely fit index is typically the first step of any analysis to determine whether or not your fund/investment is good or bad.

(There is one caveat to the above lesson, however. Sometimes portfolio managers are actually seeking a *negative correlation coefficient* to add diversification to a portfolio. For example, if you compared your fund to another investment and found they had a correlation coefficient of -100 (an R^2 equal to -1.0), then you would have found two investments that work exactly opposite of each other. When one goes up, the other goes down 100 percent of the time. And when one goes down, the other goes up 100 percent of the time. Again, finding this in real life is extremely rare, but you can seek high negative R^2 numbers if you want to consider adding a fund to create diversification in your portfolio. Sometimes you want investments that move in opposite directions to add stability to the overall performance of a portfolio. Think of these as two very different types of fruit in your fruit basket.)

If you are already disinterested in this stuff and/or are finding this overwhelming, then you are a good candidate to work with a financial advisor. You should seriously consider hiring someone to do this work for you.

Step 2: Now that you have found an index that correlates to your investment, then you can start to examine the other statistics. Your next stop: *beta.*

Beta is the statistical measurement of how fast your fund moves relative to how fast the second portfolio moves. Just because two portfolios have a high correlation coefficient (R^2) doesn't mean that they move to the same degree. Two funds could have a very high correlation coefficient, in that they almost always move in the same direction, but one fund may move much slower than the other fund.

A beta of 1.0 means that the two funds move at exactly the same speed. A beta of 0.50 means that one fund is moving at exactly half the speed of the other investment/index you are comparing it to.

In general, beta is used as a statistic to measure how risky a fund is when compared to an index. If your fund has a beta of 0.50, then you are only expecting it to move up and down about half as much as the index that you are comparing it to. Because it doesn't move as fast, you are considered to be taking less risk.

Imagine that you had two roller coasters right next to each other. One coaster is your investment, and the other coaster is the index. If you have a beta of 1.0, then both coasters look pretty similar—they have the same highs and the same lows. If, however, you have a beta of 0.50, then your roller coaster's highs and lows are exactly half as large as the index's highs and lows. On the other hand, if your coaster has a beta of 2.0, then your coaster has highs and lows that are twice as high and low as the index that you are comparing your investment to. Yep, that's right; you can invest in more aggressive funds that are taking more risk than the index. If you do, you should see a beta that is greater than 1.0.

Before you determine if your fund/investment is good or bad, you have to consider how much risk your fund is taking versus the index you are comparing it to. This is what beta is all about.

Step 3: Now that you have found the most closely fit index and determined how much risk your investment is taking, it is time to look at your expected return. Expected return is shown by the letter k in the following simplified equation:

$$k = (beta) \times (index\ rate\ of\ return)$$

In other words, you should expect your rate of return to be very similar to the performance of the closely fit index *modified by how much risk you are taking.* To stay with our roller coaster analogy, it isn't fair to expect your roller coaster car to go just as high (or just as low) as the giant coaster next to you if your coaster is only half as big. Let's take this through a quick math example.

If the index you are comparing your fund to got a rate of return of 10 percent and your investment has a beta of 0.8, then your expected rate of return (k) should be—yep—8 percent. On the other hand, if your investment had a beta of 1.2 (meaning that your roller coaster was riskier with higher highs and lower lows), then you should have an expected rate of return (k) of 12 percent!

We are so close to determining whether or not a fund is good or bad—just one more primary step to go.

Step 4: Now that you know what your expected rate of return should be, all you have to do is look at your actual rate of return and compare it to your expected rate of return. If you got a higher return than the expected rate of return, then that is good. If you got a lower rate of return than the expected rate of return, then that is bad.

So is there a number that tells us whether or not the return was better or worse than the expected return? Yes. That statistic is called *alpha.* Alpha measures how much a fund performed above or below its expected return (k). For example, if the fund above had an alpha of 2.0, then your fund performed 2 percent better than the expected return.

Imagine that your fund has a beta of 0.8. Now imagine that the index you are comparing your fund to got a 10 percent rate of return and that your fund also got a 10 percent rate of return. You might think that you just *tied* the index, but you actually got extremely good performance! You got a 10 percent rate of return, and you only took 80 percent of the risk!

Let's carry this through to the roller coaster analogy. Imagine that your coaster's highs and lows are only 80 percent as high and low as the bigger coaster (index) right next to you. Now you have a roller coaster operator who can affect the speed of your coaster by accelerating or decelerating your coaster when they think they can help you get to the end of the track faster. In spite of the fact that you are on a much safer, smaller roller coaster, the roller coaster operator was able to manually speed up your car as they operated it such that you arrived at the end of your coaster at the exact same time as the larger, faster, riskier coaster. That deserves some applause or at least a nod to the operator. Pretty cool work.

Now, it is quite possible to have negative alpha as well. What if you were on the bigger, riskier coaster with a beta of 1.2? You took more risk, and you got more scared, so you deserve a bigger reward. Your expected rate of return is 12 percent, but your roller coaster operator messed up when they were trying to help you. Instead of helping you, they actually slowed you down when you could have gone faster. Because of that, their alpha was -2.0. You got the same 10 percent rate of return, but you took 20 percent more risk! Did you even notice? Did you tell your roller coaster operator to do a better job? Did you fire that investment manager and hire one with a better track record?

Many investment companies have picked up on this statistic as a way to measure how good a job your portfolio manager is doing. If you look at the statistic alpha net of fees, then you can measure how good a job this portfolio manager did when managing your portfolio.

Remember the apple picker in the orchard above? You had to pay the second apple picker to think. If that barrel produced a positive alpha net of fees, then the apple picker added value to your account. By thinking and making good choices as apples were selected from different trees the second picker was able to successfully overperform the higher cost for his or her work (the management fees).

On another side note, it is unreasonable to consider a financial advisor's fee as a part of the investment expense above unless your advisor's primary job is to pick individual securities (how many apples from which trees in the orchard). Financial advisors are often compensated by receiving a percentage of the assets under advisement. When this is the case, their advice can often make a huge impact on your overall savings. Financial advisors often save their clients significant money by reducing taxes; they protect their clients' assets in the event of financial catastrophes; they assist with beneficiary and ownership titling; they provide the structure, implementation strategy, and monitoring for an overall financial plan; they assist with optimal account selection; AND they often help build clients' fruit baskets! If, on the other hand, the only thing your advisor does for you is manage your money, then their fee *should* be considered a part of the portfolio expense when performing your statistical analysis.

Also, remember that *each of your investments* (every individual stock, mutual fund, bond fund, bond, ETF, etc.) must be individually evaluated against its most closely fit index to make the above determinations. You will not likely have a high correlation coefficient with a single index for most diversified portfolios. You must examine each individual part within the portfolio to determine the health of the overall asset allocation.

(Of course, whether or not an examined fund is actually good or bad is a judgment call that you now have to make. Maybe this was a short-term underperformance that has good reason, and you expect the fund to do better in the future. Or, maybe a portfolio manager changed, and these statistics represented the old manager's choices. Maybe the investment objective of the fund was adjusted and the index you are comparing your fund to used to have a stronger correlation coefficient than you expect it to have going forward. There are a multitude of reasons and rationalizations to consider as you ultimately decide whether a fund is good or bad. Even after you judge a fund, you still have to decide if you intend to keep using it, with how much, and for how long.)

*How are fixed investments different from
variable investments? (Pyramid of Risk, accounts
on deposit versus separate accounts)*

The easiest way to answer this question is with a diagram.

As you can see above, there are basically three different ways to invest. The bottom of the pyramid represents the safest, most conservative way to invest. The middle area represents a slightly riskier way of investing. Finally, the top part of the pyramid represents the riskiest way of investing.

It's fine to use whatever parts of this pyramid that you would like as you evaluate your own risk tolerance and grow your wealth. However, we have learned over the years that our clients who approach retirement often move more of their assets to the safer investments at the bottom of the pyramid, and they usually have fewer investments near the top.

Let's start with an explanation of the types of investments we would find in the bottom of the pyramid.

Fixed Investments

1. With these types of investments, you can put your money on deposit with another company (typically a bank or an insurance company). That money is placed in the general account of the company, and the bank or insurance company guarantees you that they will give you some benefits for putting your money on deposit with them. Typically, these benefits could be any combination of the following: guaranteeing your money back, various amounts of interest earnings, check-writing privileges, guaranteed income benefits, and/or other insurance benefits.

   These fixed investments are the lowest-risk types of investments that you can choose. The company that your money is on deposit with is making a contractual agreement with you that you can hold them responsible for in a court of law. They make this agreement with you so that they can use your money to invest for their own benefit, and they are providing you with the benefits that they promise by using some of the money that they earn from their investment success.

   Some examples of these fixed investments would include checking accounts, savings accounts, certificates of deposit (CDs), fixed annuities, fixed index annuities, whole life insurance, universal life insurance, and indexed universal life insurance.

Variable Investments

2. As we move up the pyramid, the next level of risk involves you actually owning a group of stocks and/or

bonds. Rather than receiving the safety of a contractual guarantee, you are assuming the risk associated with ownership of actual securities yourself. These assets are *not* placed on deposit with the company. The company you invest with is *not* contractually guaranteeing that you will receive any benefits. Your protection in this type of investment is gained largely through *professional management* and your hope in the theory of *diversification*.

Your money is placed in a *separate account* where the actual securities are purchased and held for your benefit. You typically own a wide variety of securities. You may actually have a portfolio that includes hundreds if not thousands of different securities from all over the world. These portfolios typically come with the professional management of a portfolio manager or a team of managers.

Some examples of these types of investments would include stock mutual funds, bond mutual funds, index funds, ETFs, and variable annuities.[33]

Individual Securities and Direct Ownership

3. The final, top part of the pyramid represents the riskiest investment strategies. Here we remove the professional

---

[33] Variable annuities can function as a hybrid between this middle category of the pyramid and the bottom category of the pyramid if you add contractual guarantees (like living benefits). However, variable annuity investments are more similar to the other investments in the middle part of the pyramid in that money in these accounts is invested in a separate account with professional management and a wide variety of securities attempting to benefit from diversification.

money management and/or the diversification. When you choose individual, direct ownership, you are assuming the most risk. Of course, with greater risk you have the potential of a greater reward, but you risk greater losses (including the possible loss of everything you have invested).

Examples of these types of investments include stocks, bonds, direct ownership in real estate, cryptocurrency, limited partnerships, private businesses, and certain alternative investments.

We would recommend that you plot your own wealth on the pyramid of risk. See how much of your net worth is invested in these various risk classes. There truly is no right or wrong; you can build your pyramid however you like. Of course, we believe that building your portfolio with the assistance of a professional financial advisor will likely help you improve your performance through increased safety, increased performance, or possibly both.

What is the difference between tax-deductible, tax-deferred, and tax-free? Also, what's the difference between a Roth 401k/IRA and a Regular 401k/IRA?

Taxes! That word almost always has an exclamation point after it, or at least some kind of emotion when discussed. These three strategies, however—tax deductibility, tax-deferred growth, and tax-free access—are three ways to legally shrink your tax bill. So how are they different?

Let's start with tax deductibility.

Each and every year you are in a partnership with your government. When you live somewhere with public benefits you have to chip in to help pay for all the public services that your government provides. This includes a multitude of services that many of us take for granted. Everything that benefits the entire population is typically paid for completely or partially by the government. This includes police officers, firefighters, teachers, prisons, road construction, national parks, and the military (just to name a few).

Usually you have to make income tax payments to your government on an ongoing basis. Most employees do this by having federal (and state if applicable) income taxes withheld from their paychecks. Self-employed people and retirees who may not have a regular paycheck often have to send estimated tax payments at specified times during the year. Finally, at the end of the year, we all file our income tax return.

The purpose of your annual tax filing is to *true up* or *settle* your tax bill. The ultimate annual bill for your taxes varies depending on a wide variety of factors (how much money you made, your marital status, your age, where and how you earned your money, what kind of expenses you had, etc.). A calculation needs to be done to see how much you were supposed to pay for your right to benefit from the services the government provides; the form for doing that calculation is your tax return.

If it turns out that you paid more than you owed, then you get a refund of your overpayment. On the other hand, if you didn't pay enough during the year, then you need to settle up and pay the money that you owe your government.

Tax deductibility is a way that the government acknowledges they like something that you spent money on. When you spend money on something that results in a tax deduction, the government lets you exclude it from your income when they total up your annual bill.

Here is an example:

Let's assume that you received $100,000 in income last year. Now let's imagine that you had a $10,000 *tax deduction*. The government lets you *subtract* that $10,000 from your income for that year *before* you have to calculate the money that you owe for taxes. That's right—it's like you were able to make that money *legally invisible* when it came to paying your tax bill!

If you were in a 22 percent tax bracket and didn't have that $10,000 tax deduction, then you would have had to pay $2,200 *extra* because of that $10,000 of income you received last year. But, because you had a $10,000 tax deduction, you saved $2,200 in federal income taxes. If you were in a higher tax bracket, then you may have saved even more. Furthermore, if your state also recognizes the same $10,000 tax deduction, then you may have saved even more money by reducing your state income tax bill.

So what does *tax-deferred growth* mean?

To explain tax-deferred growth, we need to talk about investment earnings. The easiest example for us to discuss is something most people are pretty familiar with: a savings account.

(I know that interest rates on savings accounts haven't been very high lately—as this book is being written, interest rates on savings accounts are often well below 1 percent per year—but we can still use this to better understand tax-deferred growth.)

Imagine that you have $100,000 invested in a savings account that is earning 1 percent interest per year. This means that you earned $1,000 in interest at the end of the year. If you earned that 1 percent inside a regular savings account, then you will get a 1099 form from your bank at the end of the year. A copy of this form is sent to you as well as to the federal government. (That way the federal government knows that you received that $1,000, and they can expect you to report it on your tax return and pay taxes accordingly.) Under current tax law, that $1,000 in interest earned on a regular savings account is not tax deductible. This means that you have to report that $1,000 on your taxes and pay the appropriate amount of taxes on that income.

If, however, you had that $100,000 inside a tax-deferred investment account (like a 401k, IRA, nonqualified annuity, or life insurance policy), then you would not have had to report those earnings on your tax return this year. The full $1,000 would have been added to your investment account balance at the end of the year with *no* tax consequences! Then you would (presumably) be able to reinvest those earnings and earn interest on those earnings the following year.

Imagine if that investment had paid 10 percent interest. Then $100,000 would have grown to $110,000 and you wouldn't have had to pay taxes on that $10,000 of earnings if it was in a tax-deferred investment account!

If you do this over many years (like over an entire working career in a 401k, for example) you can continue to earn interest on the tax dollars that would have otherwise had to be paid to your government. This has the potential to snowball your earnings into a much larger nest egg when you are eventually ready to retire.

So what about tax-free access?

Most of the tax-deferred investment accounts mentioned above will result in you *eventually* having to pay taxes on that money. As you are probably aware by now, when you draw money from your regular 401k account in retirement, you will have to report that money to the IRS and pay taxes. However, there are a few special types of investment accounts that produce tax-free distributions.

Roth 401k's, Roth IRAs, and 529 plans all offer the ability to draw out earnings that *have never been taxed before without having to pay ANY income taxes when you follow their rules upon making withdrawals!* (To be clear, your contributions to the Roth IRA, Roth 401k, and 529 plans are made with *after-tax* dollars. Therefore, your *contributions* have already been taxed. The money that has never been taxed is the *earnings* made within these types of accounts.)

According to current tax law, if you withdraw money from a Roth 401k or Roth IRA after the age of fifty-nine and a half, then *ALL* those withdrawals are *tax-free*. This means that you could have grown thousands or even millions of dollars inside these accounts over the years that have never been taxed; then you get to spend that money without paying taxes on it later in retirement! Of course, when the government gives you these kinds of benefits, they also put some limits on them. There are limits on how much money you can contribute to a Roth IRA and a Roth 401k. There is also a five-year minimum holding period on certain Roth conversions before you can make tax-free withdrawals from these types of accounts. Make sure that you seek guidance from your financial advisor and/or tax professional before investing in these accounts so that you thoroughly understand these limits and the rules for tax-free withdrawal.

Similarly, tax-free withdrawals from 529 plans are allowed as long as they are made for qualifying educational expenses for the designated beneficiary. The rules for these qualifying educational expenses were recently expanded under the Tax Cuts and Jobs Act of 2017. If a designated beneficiary doesn't use the money, then the owner can always change the beneficiary to another individual (including the owner) to help with that person's education expenses. Options were further expanded with the SECURE ACT 2.0 to allow for certain qualifying unused funds to be rolled into a beneficiary's ROTH IRA. Again, if withdrawals are taken out for nonqualifying expenses, then there are penalties. Please consult with a professional before choosing this type of investment for education funding.

Finally, loans on certain types of life insurance are also tax-free. One strategy that is commonly used with life insurance is to build a significant amount of cash value inside these tax-deferred investment vehicles. Then, rather than withdrawing the earnings and paying taxes, the owner of the policy can take tax-free loans from the policy. Finally, rather than paying back the loans during their lifetime, the owner allows the income tax–free death benefit to pay off the loan when the insured finally passes away. Again, these types of tax-deferred investment vehicles and loan strategies are complicated and often require the guidance of a financial advisor and/or an insurance professional.[34]

---

[34] Like the Roth 401k, Roth IRA, and 529 plans mentioned above, contributions made to most life insurance policies are made with money that has already been taxed. Also, there are certain circumstances when life insurance death benefits can be taxable; be sure to work with an insurance professional and tax professional when you use life insurance policies in this manner.

What's the difference between income taxes,
capital gains taxes, and estate taxes?

Taxes *again?* I know—there is a lot to learn. For many people taxes are one of their biggest annual expenses. When you look at how much you pay in taxes in a given year, it is a sizable amount. Taking a little bit of time to learn the basics could save you thousands if not millions of dollars over your lifetime.

We focused on income taxes when we went through tax deductibility, tax-deferred growth, and tax-free access above. All those strategies are primarily designed to legally reduce or avoid income taxes.

Income taxes are the taxes that you pay each year based on how much income you received. They are charged on a *progressive* tax structure. This means that the more taxable income you receive, the higher the percentage that you pay in income taxes.

A common *misconception* about income taxes is the idea that the tax brackets will somehow be retroactive. This is *not* the case. Let me explain with this example.

Let's consider a married couple earning taxable income of $85,000 per year. That puts them in the marginal tax bracket of 12 percent on their federal tax return. This means that for the last $1,000 that they received, they paid $120 (12 percent) in federal taxes. Many people that I have spoken with have been deathly afraid of making enough money that they end up in the next tax bracket. In this case, another $5,000 in that tax year would put this couple in the 22 percent tax bracket. (The cutoff for a married couple filing jointly in 2023 is $89,450.)

The fear is that if their taxable income goes up to $90,000 (just into the next bracket), then this poor married couple will now need to pay 22 percent in taxes on the whole of their $90,000 income, which would amount to an extra $9000 in taxes!

Don't worry! As I said above, this is a common *misconception*. The reality is that you will only pay taxes at the 22 percent rate on the portion of income that is over the $89,450 limit. This couple only pays the 22 percent tax rate on $550 of income if they earn $90,000. They still pay the lower tax rates on the income below $89,450!

This misconception has led people to work terribly hard to keep their income under these threshold amounts. Some people will even stop working near the end of the year out of fear that they will *earn too much!* Sadly, all that energy could have been spent on better endeavors.

What this progressive tax structure does mean, however, is that *everyone* benefits from the lower tax brackets. Everyone (even the highest income earners) receive lower tax bills on the money they earn in the lowest tax brackets.

So where do capital gains taxes fit in?

Capital gains tax is a completely different kind of tax. Capital gains tax is the tax you owe because something that you bought went up in value between the time you bought it and the time you sold it.

For example:

Imagine that you bought a painting for $1,000 a few years ago. Since then, the artist has grown famous. Now, your painting is worth $25,000. What a wonderful windfall.

You don't have to pay taxes on the painting until you actually sell the painting and realize the gain on that painting. But if you sell it, then the IRS says that you owe taxes on the difference between what you paid for it ($1,000) and what you sold it for ($25,000). Therefore, they say that you owe taxes on $24,000.

Fortunately, the IRS gives you preferential tax treatment on this $24,000. In general, the United States *likes the idea of you investing*. So if your overall income is low enough, you may owe 0 percent federal taxes on that $24,000 gain. If, however, you are married filing jointly with taxable income above $89,250, then you will pay 15 percent long-term capital gains taxes on your realized capital gain in that year. If your taxable income is above $553,850, then the long-term capital gains rate is 20 percent. This is still *much lower* than the regular income tax rates at these income levels.

These preferential rates only apply to assets that you purchased and held for one year or longer. If you sell an asset in less than a year, then your gains are considered *short-term capital gains* and are subject to regular income tax rates. There are also special provisions for the sale of your primary residence, and there are ways to postpone long-term capital gains tax consequences for other assets if you follow certain tax strategies (this includes strategies like 1031 exchanges, etc.). Again, to pursue any of these advanced tax strategies, we recommend that you speak with a tax professional and/or a financial advisor about your unique circumstances.

Finally, we have *estate taxes*.

Estate taxes are a tax that the federal government applies when you transfer your wealth from one generation to the next. At certain levels, this tax can be higher than 50 percent of the wealth being transferred!

Fortunately, the Tax Cuts and Jobs Act of 2017 increased the amount of wealth that one family can transfer down to their children without incurring this significant tax. Based on the current tax code, each individual (with proper planning) can pass down a little over $12.92 million without paying a federal estate tax. With good planning, there are ways to legally avoid taxes for a married couple on a little over $25.84 million of an estate. (If your estate appears to be greater than this number, then you definitely want to consult with financial planners, attorneys, and tax professionals to have a plan in place to legally minimize your estate tax bill. Furthermore, you should consider which assets will be the best assets to pay this tax when you pass away, as the bill is due nine months after death. And many investors with this kind of net worth do not have enough of it liquid within nine months of death at reasonable values. Many times, the heirs are forced to have a *fire sale* where many assets are sold below their real value, and much of an estate can be lost. Often times, the best asset to pay this tax bill is a life insurance policy placed in an irrevocable life insurance trust (ILIT) so that its death benefit is not also included in the estate of the family who passed.)

If you were reading this and thinking, *Whew, I'm off the hook. Don't have that kind of money. Wish I had that kind of problem*, you're not off the hook yet. This particular increase from the Tax Cuts and Jobs Act of 2017 goes away at the end of 2025! Unless you know *for sure* that you (and your spouse, if applicable) will pass away in the next few years, then planning for estate taxes is still extremely important.

Finally, even though the federal thresholds are this high, many states have *much lower* thresholds. Oregon, for example (where I live), only exempts $1 million per person before they charge estate taxes on everything over that. There are a lot more people with $1 million than there are with $12.92 million. Be sure to know the estate taxes in your state and/or country. There are countless stories of famous people who died with a significant amount of wealth only to pass on a pittance of that wealth due to poor estate tax planning.

What about property taxes, sales tax, gift taxes, and generation-skipping tax?

I know; you're like—*We get it. There are a lot of taxes.* This part will be brief. If you want to keep your taxes at a minimum, you just have to do two things: (1) Learn more about taxes. (2) Work with a tax professional who knows more than you do about taxes.

Property taxes: Tax that you pay (usually to your city, county, or state) because you own certain types of property (usually real estate).

Sales tax: Commonly assessed in many states to help with revenue. This is a tax typically on goods and/or services bought in your state to help fund government agencies at a state level. Some states have a very high sales tax and no income tax. Other states have a higher income tax and no sales tax. Still, many states collect revenue from both a sales tax and an income tax.

Gift tax: Federally, the estate tax bill is also tied to gift taxes. (The IRS doesn't want you just giving away $100 million right before you die making them unable to collect the estate tax on that.) The tax code is tied into the estate tax so that you can usually gift away a similar amount during life as you can upon death. When you give a gift, the IRS wants you to file a gift tax return so they can track how much you have given away during your lifetime. Then they settle up with your estate when you die. If you give away a small enough amount each year (currently $17,000 per person), then you don't have to report this gift on a gift tax return. If you give more, however, you are supposed to file that gift tax return. Again, check with your tax professional for state rules and more details on the federal rules.

Generation-skipping tax: Be careful if you try to pass money directly to grandkids and great-grandkids. If it's too much money, then the IRS gets to look at it as if it is subject to two transfers. Look at it this way: they don't want to miss out on the estate taxes they could have charged your kids to pass the money to your grandkids. Again, work with a professional. These rules, and the best strategies, are constantly in flux.

What's the difference between Medicare and Medicaid?

I'm so glad you asked! This is another commonly misunderstood issue.

Medicare is the federal health insurance that all US citizens are eligible to receive once they turn age sixty-five or become disabled.

This is a basic level of health insurance. It does not cover many things that many employee group health insurance plans cover. To upgrade this insurance, most people choose to supplement this coverage with a *Medigap* policy (a separate policy purchased to fill in the gaps of basic Medicare), a *Medicare Advantage Plan* (a plan that replaces your basic coverage with a more comprehensive plan that is subsidized by the federal government), or another form of health insurance.

Even with the most comprehensive Medigap policy, the most comprehensive Medicare Advantage Policy, and the best supplemental health insurance plans, none of them will cover long-term care expenses for more than one hundred days.

Long-term care costs are one of the biggest financial risks facing our retiring baby boomer community over the years ahead. It is critical to make a conscious, informed decision about how you and your family want to handle this risk. There are many strategies to address this, and the marketplace has evolved significantly over the past forty years. If you haven't looked at this risk and ways to protect against it in the last three years, you should review this with your financial professional(s).

Medicaid is the federally funded plan that pays for US citizens when they have *no other resources* to pay for themselves. Bottom line: This is only for when you are broke!

Currently, Medicaid only allows you to benefit when your life savings are down to $2,000 and your primary home equity. (No, I didn't forget a zero or two.) If you are married, they will typically allow your spouse to retain at most $148,620 of "Countable Assets" and up to a maximum of $688,000 of your primary home equity. If you have more than $100,000 in assets, you should plan to learn more about the risk of long-term care costs and make a decision as to how you will handle this. There are many rules in place to force people to use their wealth before the federal government picks up the tab. If you are thinking that you have a way around this, be sure that you have spoken with a long-term care attorney, Medicaid planning attorney, and/or an elder law attorney to be sure that your strategy will work. Also, like tax codes, these rules are also constantly changing. Stay current on your plan.

When should I take my Social Security?

I almost didn't put this question in here. I know that it is one of the most important questions that many of my readers will be asking, but the answer to this is so complicated I could write a separate book on this topic alone.

But I'm not going to leave you hanging. Let's take a crack at some of the bottom-line problems and give you some insights as to why it's so complicated and hard to answer.

The first problem with answering this question is that the right answer is different *for everyone!* I know; you don't want to hear that. It feels like a cop-out. And it kind of is. So here we go at some generalizations. I won't tell you a definitive "this is what you should do," but I will make it easier for you to figure out your own answer. And, again, I encourage you to discuss this one with your financial advisor and the Social Security Administration.

The biggest reason why I can't answer this universally for everyone is because I don't know when you are going to die. If you told me when you were going to die, I could calculate the best answer down to the penny. But let's go a little deeper.

Social Security was designed to protect people who became disabled and to provide for the elderly if they happened to live a few years longer than average. When it was designed it wasn't created with the expectation that we would all live as long as we are living today. It is a pay-as-you-go system, meaning that the government taxes those who are still actively employed, and it turns around and pays that money to those who are retired and receiving Social Security benefits. That's right—the money is essentially taken from the working class and paid to retirees.

Now, over the years, retirees have grown to feel that they truly deserve this money. After all, for their entire working careers they gave part of their paychecks to the people who have been collecting retirement Social Security benefits. Like a pyramid scheme, those who were early into the program benefited the most. The first recipients of Social Security income paid in for one or two paychecks and, in many cases, reaped the rewards of Social Security for years. If Social Security comes crashing down, then all the people who paid into it their whole lives would be left holding the bag—just like the last people to enter a pyramid scheme.

I don't want to worry you that Social Security will all come crashing down. I believe the most likely solution for the Social Security dilemma is that taxes will go up on workers to pay for retirees. Currently, Social Security taxes are seen as a line item on everyone's paycheck under the acronym FICA. The tax for this is 6.2 percent paid from employees, and that is matched by another 6.2 percent paid by the employers. (Yep, if you are an employee, your employer is paying an extra 6.2 percent of your earnings to the government as Social Security taxes.) If you are self-employed, you know the Social Security tax under the name self-employment taxes, which are currently 15.3 percent. That 15.3 percent breaks down as follows: 6.2 percent for the employee side of FICA, 6.2 percent for the employer side of FICA, 1.45 percent for the employee side of Medicare taxes, and 1.45 percent for the employer side of Medicare taxes. The good news: once you hit the maximum wage base for Social Security taxes (currently $160,200 per person in 2023), you pay only the Medicare tax. (Of course, a

Medicare surcharge tax has been added to your annual tax bill when your income goes to higher levels. This is because the costs for Medicare, Medicaid, and Social Security are so far beyond what was anticipated when these were put into place that tax increases have become inevitable, and those increases have already begun.) This is why I would say that the most likely short-term solution to the Social Security problem will be an increase in taxes on those who make over the $160,200 wage base. After all, they are a minority, and it is the majority of the public that votes a politician/legislator into office.

But let's get back to answering your question. If we assume that the rules for Social Security don't change by the time you read this (a big assumption), then you are currently eligible to receive Social Security benefits at sixty-two years old. You would receive a reduced amount; your full amount is only received if you wait till your normal retirement age. Depending on your birth year, this is either sixty-six years old, sixty-seven years old, or somewhere in between.

If you take Social Security income before your normal retirement age, then you will experience a reduction in your benefits based on how many months early you took your benefit. (That's right, every month that you delay, your benefit goes up a little bit.) Also, if you take it before you reach normal retirement age, then you will lose a dollar of Social Security income for every two dollars that you earn over an annual wage limit (the limit is currently set at a little over $21,240.) So if you are still working and making a decent income, it will usually not make sense for you to take Social Security benefits early. If you are not earning more than $21,240, then you have to do more math to see if it makes sense to take your Social Security benefits early.

The biggest additional insight that can help you with this question will come from how you answer this question: Do you need the Social Security income?

If, like most Americans, you will be dependent on your Social Security income to survive in retirement, then it is usually in your best interest to wait as long as you can before you turn on your Social Security benefits. You can continue to get increases in your lifetime Social Security benefits for each month you wait to start it until you reach age seventy.

If your answer to "Do you need it?" was "No, but I want it," then you are probably trying to solve a different math problem than the majority of retiring Americans. You are trying to get *the most* out of Social Security.

The majority of my clients have sought my help to answer this question. The answer truly depends on each client's situation. How healthy are you? How healthy is your spouse? How will you and your family feel if you are wrong about your life expectancy?

Look at the quick math. If you stop working at sixty (i.e., you retire early) and you die at seventy, you would obviously collect more money by taking your Social Security benefits at sixty-two years old. You have to look at how many years you would receive the benefit as well as how much the benefit is.

On the other hand, if you live to ninety-five years old, then the amount of Social Security income that you would collect after waiting until age seventy (to get the maximum increase possible) will result in you having collected much more money between seventy and ninety-five at the higher amount versus collecting a lower amount between age sixty-two and ninety-five.

There are a lot of assumptions that go into any analysis of this question. The bottom line: If you pass away before eighty, you are usually better off having taken it early. If you live past ninety-five, you are usually better having waited. If you die somewhere in the middle, it depends on the assumptions you made in your analysis.

Once you make this decision, it's pretty final. I recommend that you discuss this decision with a financial advisor and ensure you make a well-informed choice before you lock this in.

What's the deal with required minimum distributions (RMDs) and inherited/beneficiary IRAs?

So either you've inherited an IRA or you are approaching seventy-three years old and have heard about something called RMDs. (Or you just like to learn about stuff that doesn't affect you yet but might one day.)

The required minimum distribution (RMD), like many of these questions, is another income tax issue.

The bottom line: the government gave you a big tax deduction on those 401k contributions all those years ago, and they are tired of waiting to collect their share. You went into partnership with the IRS when you decided to put pretax money into your 401k. They said, "Okay, we won't tax you on this money that is going into your 401k because we want you to save for yourself in retirement. But you can't just keep pushing off the tax bill forever." This is where the seventy-three RMD rule comes into play.

Once people turn seventy-three years old in the United States, they have reached the point where the IRS says they must start taking money out of their 401k's, IRAs, and other qualified retirement plans. (Note: these RMDs are not required on Roth IRAs and Roth 401k's. This is because the IRS isn't due any taxes on these Roth distributions.)

So how much do you have to take out?

To determine how much you need to take out of your retirement plans to comply with the RMD rules, you need to do some math. There is a special table that the IRS publishes. Based on your age, you take the balance of your qualified retirement plan accounts as of December 31 of the year *prior* to the year that you turn seventy-three and divide it by the number in the table. You must then withdraw that amount before April 1 of the year *following* the year in which you turn seventy-three. This is only for your first RMD distribution.

Once you get into the second year of RMDs, you need to take your newly calculated RMD before December 31 of the year *after* you turn seventy-three. Going forward, you must take your RMD prior to December 31 each and every year, and the amount you must take is based on an ever-increasing percentage of the prior year's December 31 value. Again, this is obtained from the IRS-published table. (Note: If you have an annuity with additional benefits, your RMD may be affected. You may need to take a slightly greater amount than the simple fraction of your account value because of the extra financial benefits that the annuity may offer you. Be sure to seek the help of your financial advisor, tax professional, and/or the insurance company that you have your annuity contract invested with.)

The tax penalty if you don't take out your RMD is 25 percent of whatever you were supposed to take out but didn't. I know—that's a lot! Don't mess this one up, because that's a lot of tax penalties. This reason alone is a good reason to make sure that you are working with a financial advisor and a tax professional. One year of messing this up could have been enough to cover the costs of your financial advisor and/or your tax professional for several years of service! You should also talk to them about qualified charitable donations (QCDs) and possibly donor-advised funds if you are charitably inclined.

So why do inherited IRAs (also known as beneficiary IRAs) also fit in the answer to this question? That's because they often have RMDs as well.

If you are the recipient of an inherited IRA, then you will have some distribution choices to consider. First of all, if you inherit the IRA (or 401k) from your spouse, then you have the option of moving the asset into an IRA in your own name and merging it with any other IRA or 401k assets that you may have. Often times this choice works out very well, but there *are* some circumstances when you *would not* want to do this. For example, if your spouse has passed away and left you an IRA or 401k balance and you merge it into your own IRA or 401k account, then your inheritance will now be subject to the fifty-nine-and-a-half / 10 percent penalty rule. If you inherit this account when you are under the age of fifty-nine and a half and need access to it, you may want to choose one of the other distribution options.

If you inherit an IRA or 401k account from a person who is not your spouse—or you are the spouse and you choose not to merge the inherited IRA/401k into your own IRA/401k—then you will now have to set up an inherited/beneficiary IRA account in your own name.

Because the IRS doesn't want you to simply postpone those tax consequences on your newly inherited IRA, they force you to take the money out by no later than ten years after inheritance. Sadly, this also applies to inherited ROTH IRA's. This new change to inherited IRA's was implemented by the SECURE Act in 2019 to stop the tax benefits received from the old stretch IRA and stretch ROTH IRA concepts. Those strategies are no longer viable for IRA's inherited in 2020 and later. (If you inherited an IRA or a ROTH IRA in 2019 or earlier, then the stretch IRA strategy can still be used on these assets.)

Additionally, after some debate, the rules of the 2019 SECURE ACT were further interpreted such that annual RMD requirements must still be met on inherited IRA's up until the account is fully liquidated by the end of the ten years. If you have an inherited IRA it is important to stay up to date on these recently changed rules and regulations to avoid any penalty taxes.

Of course, like any of the above suggestions/ideas, everyone's situation is different. You should consult with a financial advisor, an attorney, and a tax professional whenever you are unsure of what financial decision you want to make.

INDEX

n denotes footnote

A

accounts
  checking, 107
  401k. See 401k
  403b, 52, 53–54
  with guarantees, 30
  IRA (individual retirement
    account). See IRA
    (individual retirement
    account)
  savings, 33, 34, 107, 112
  separate, 108
  without guarantees, 30
accumulation years, 25
actively managed funds, 90,
  91–92, 98
age-weighted funds, 96
alpha, 99, 102–104
alternative investments, 34, 109
AMEX (American Stock
  Exchange) (now NYSE
  American), 23, 87
annuities

as attracting attention
  of more and more
  investors, 56
bad rep of in '90s, 54
basic strategy of, 37–38
as complicated, 59, 60
deciding how much to put
  into one, 63–71
defined, 38
evolution of, 43–62
fixed annuities, 38n13
increase in sales of over last
  two decades, 62
indexed annuities, 38n13
innovations in, 55, 56
joint-and-survivor
  annuitization
  option, 49
liquidity of, 63–64
negative spotlight to, 50
pros and cons of, 63
scenarios about, 43–52
single premium immediate
  annuity (SPIA), 45–
  46, 48

on taking money out of
401ks, 8
international funds, as
compared with S&P
500, 93
investing
alternative investments,
34, 109
belief of in timing the
market, 80
bucket approach/bucket
strategy to, 30, 32–35
buy and hold strategy to,
80–82
fixed investments, 107
guaranteed approach to,
37–39
non-guaranteed approach
to, 31–35
questions about with
easy-to-understand
answers, 77–80, 85, 86,
90, 95, 98, 106, 110, 116,
121, 123, 125, 130
strategic investing, 80–82
tactical investing, 82–84
taking a new approach to,
26–30
timing the market, 82–84
investment earnings, 112
IRA (individual retirement
account). See also Roth
IRAs
big distribution as
potentially costing

lots of money in taxes,
8, 10
inherited/beneficiary IRAs,
132–133
rolling 401k over to, 67–68
traditional IRA as one of
worst assets to leave
behind, 8
irrevocable life insurance trust
(ILIT), 119

J

joint-and-survivor annuitization
option, 49

K

k (expected rate of return),
101–102, 103

L

lagging indicators, 85
large cap, 23, 24, 98
last in first out (LIFO), 51
leading indicators, 85
legacy, leaving of, 8, 70
life insurance
as better asset to leave
behind than
traditional 401k, 8
irrevocable life insurance
trust (ILIT), 119
loans on certain types of as
tax-free, 115
universal life insurance, 107
whole life insurance, 107
liquidity, annuities and, 63–64